The Retirement Dilemma

The Bins and Gaps Method of Retirement Planning

Rick DiBiasio CFP ™

DEDICATION

I wrote much of this book while sitting with my wife of almost 30 years, Teresa, in the Florida Hospital Chemotherapy clinic or while sitting with her in our home as she suffered through the results of her cancer treatments. Teresa's strength, courage, and positive attitude have helped to lead our entire family through this crisis as she has successfully battled Stage 4 breast cancer. I begin and end every day with a simple prayer that asks that we be able to someday enjoy our own retirement years together.

ACKNOWLEDGMENTS

I am blessed to have a wonderful family who supports my creative and entrepreneurial endeavors with a knowing wink and almost no smirks. To Teresa, my daughters, Suzanne, Elizabeth, Rachel, and my son, James, thank you for your love and indulgence.

Securities and Advisory Services offered through LPL Financial, a Registered Investment Advisor, Member FINRA/ SIPC.

CONTENTS

1

INTRODUCTION

**Clowns to the left of me, jokers to the right,
here I am, stuck in the middle with you.
Steelers Wheel**

I'm a Baby Boomer, and I wanted to write this book for you because I am tired of the usual Wall Street corporate speak which usually amounts to legalize, industry jargon, and implied guilt that says, "You haven't saved enough for retirement (no matter how much you have saved for retirement) and you aren't capable of understanding all of this financial stuff anyway. Give us your money; you can trust us!" As a career financial guy, I wanted to write a book that talks about retirement planning as if we were two friends having dinner together in our favorite restaurant (I prefer Italian, what's good for you?) I want to give you some easy to grasp concepts that will help you to answer some questions like Can I retire yet? Will I run out of money? and How should I invest my retirement money? I'm probably not going to answer these questions for you specifically, but I hope to give you a methodology to answer those questions for yourself.

A short while ago, I had a new potential client call my firm, an older woman who was referred to my practice by her tax accountant. We talked for quite a while about her investment experience, and as she and I talked, like two friends, I thought everything was going fine until she said, "I think you are a great guy and someone who really takes good care of his clients, but I don't know if you are a knowledgeable enough investment guy." When I asked her what gave her that idea, she said that her present investment guy used many more technical terms and, although he left her confused, she always got the feeling that he was a lot smarter than she was about investing. I laughed, a real belly laugh, and then we had a serious talk. I explained that I had worked on Wall Street, worked for a major brokerage firm, and a bank, before I opened my own retirement planning practice. I told her I was a Certified Financial Planner ™ and then proceeded to lay on her all terms that her present guy dazzled her with: Alpha, Beta, Correlation, Monte Carlo Theory, and every other term that we Wall Street guys are taught to say. When I was done, she felt better, knowing that I actually understood my craft, and she signed the transfer forms, but only after I promised to never talk to her in anything other than plain English again.

We all remember the scene at the end of the Wizard of Oz when the Great and Powerful Oz was revealed to be nothing more than a conman; "Pay no attention to the man behind that curtain." Wall Street does that to us, using technical terms, past performance, and statistics to confuse people who have worked hard enough to save some money and have the common sense to find a professional to help manage it. I'm not going to do that. I'm going to give you a simple, common sense method of retirement analysis called the "Bins and Gaps Method." Simply, we are going to look at your anticipated retirement lifestyle and your budget and compare that to your sources of income. We'll decide if your potential income will cover your expenses and decide whether your retirement is Funded or Unfunded, and then we'll talk about what to do about that; all in common sense and plain old American-type English.

We Boomers are the first generation to retire after the great 401K experiment and we are expected to fund our retirement at a time when interest rates are at historic lows, the stock market close to record highs, and the future of the Social Security System in some question. Many of us are delaying (or giving up on) retirement and we wonder if we will ever be able to hand in our office keys and stay home for good. In *The Retirement Dilemma*, I explain how anyone can retire, regardless of assets saved, provided that they live within their means.

My experience in handling client portfolios for thirty years is this: everyone is unique. Bill and Joyce might be a whole lot like Don and Jill, but they aren't exactly alike. They might be the same age, have about the same size portfolio, and even have similar risk tolerances. But Bill and Joyce have no income needs and are remarried with a complicated estate plan. Don and Jill are in need of a monthly income and absolutely will not invest in anything that is against their social conscience. What's important to one investor often doesn't even cross another one's radar and there is no algorithm that covers every single variable. So in The Retirement Dilemma, I strive to give you some hints and guidelines to help you design a plan that is specific to your unique situation.

One of the side effects of living in a digital society is that we in danger of becoming data points ourselves. The digital world makes assumptions about us based on our credit score, our demographics, our income, and our net worth. Our lives are reduced to one big algorithm that Madison Avenue, Amazon, and, yes, Wall Street use to sell us everything from socks to nifty retirement plan strategies. So: "You are 58, married, hate risk, and have $500,000 in your IRA? You get plan #234, a perfectly personalized portfolio for you and everyone else who fills out a questionnaire similarly." Computers are awesome, aren't they? But computer driven programs are driven by historical data and mathematical formulas, not by intelligent human experience. Just as fantasy football is nothing more than a synthetic attempt to artificially re-create football, computer designed retirement plans are a mere approximation of real life. Let's get back to reality, the kind you have to face before you opt to get your gold watch. (Does anybody really get a gold watch anymore?)

So before I get further into my rant about data and robo-advisors, let's start talking about you, and your ability to retire. I hope that my efforts to write to you proves to be helpful and I advise you to look at my website: www.latitudesfinancial.com to get more information to help you pursue your retirement goals.

2

THE BOOMER'S DILEMMA

**Ain't but one way out baby,
Lord I just can't go out that door.
The Allman Brothers**

It seems that some of us spend our whole lives in "survival mode." You know what survival mode is: it's when you focus on just getting through the next day financially, physically, and emotionally. You don't thrive in survival mode; you only hope to survive in survival mode. So it's no wonder that we read about so many baby boomers not being ready to commit to living a life in retirement. While we all might like to retire to our vineyards in California or set sail across the Atlantic in our sailboats, the reality is that many baby boomers have too many questions about retirement to actually commit to walking out of our offices for the last time. After 30 years of working with people's personal finance I wrote *The Retirement Dilemma* for the people who don't think they have enough money to retire—and for the people who do. It's been my experience that everyone who retires has some concerns about living the rest of their lives without getting another paycheck, no matter how much money they have set aside.

We have all faced challenges in our lives—those days and weeks and months when we are just happy to get through each day. Sometimes we are faced with economic challenges, sometimes health problems arise, or sometimes our personal lives tumble into chaos. When we are in survival mode we aren't very creative, we aren't particularly enjoying life, and we aren't at our best. While survival mode might teach us character, we would like to think that the tough days are behind us when it comes to retirement and we hope that, at least financially, our retirement years can be years in which we thrive and not just survive. I'm not saying that you have to be wealthy or have millions of dollars to live a comfortable retirement lifestyle; I'm saying that a little retirement planning can go a long way. Ideally, you should have control over your planned retirement expenses, and the availability of funds support your lifestyle. A financially successful retirement can be summed up this simply: *you spend less than you make.*

Not long ago I had lunch with old friends and clients, a retired couple who immigrated to the United States from a communist country over 50 years ago. They arrived here with just the clothes on their backs and put their heads down and worked. They raised a beautiful and loving family and retired in their mid-sixties. In going over their finances I made sure to stop and congratulate them as their assets were now worth more than $1 million! They had achieved the American dream, something that very few people would know about them if they saw us having lunch together. They looked like the humble and loving couple that they are; not the type of people someone would pick out of a crowd as "millionaires." I should tell you this about them too: they had done such a good job taking care of their finances that they can meet their monthly living expenses simply from their Social Security payments. Their humble lifestyle is part of who they are; they have learned to live within their means at an early age. The message, at least for me, is that living within your means is the key to financial success, and this book is largely based on that premise.

We Americans are pretty good at borrowing money and worrying about how we'll pay for things later, which is fine as far as it goes, but it pretty much won't work in retirement. In *The Retirement Dilemma*, we'll talk about the income that will come to you for the rest of your life, like Social Security payments, and compare them to your monthly expenses. We will talk about what to do if you have a gap between your guaranteed income payments and your budget and what to do if you don't. We're going to talk about ways to maximize Social Security, how to make good choices with your other pension type payments (if you have any), and how to determine if your retirement account assets are substantial enough to fill your monthly gap for the rest of your life. We'll talk extensively about investing (and speculating), what happens to your IRA accounts as you get older, and how to set up your estate. But; most importantly, I hope to help you find the confidence to pull the trigger on retirement and begin the great second act of life that we all hope our retirement will be.

Investment Expertise Required

So here's what they wanted us to do: They wanted us to sustain a career; raise our families; put our kids through college; buy and pay for a house; get ourselves through divorces, health issues, and everything else we are supposed to pay for during adulthood; and, oh yeah, save enough money so that we can become financially independent and never collect another paycheck again as we face the real possibility, thanks to great medical breakthroughs, that we might live to be 100 years old. And in the interest of science we want you to manage your own money and navigate the lowest interest rates since the Great Depression while the stock market is close to record high valuations.

No problem, right? You got this? Well, I'll tell you what, I'm a professional investment guy and this scenario has been on my mind for about a decade now, and I am so concerned about it that I actually sat down to write this book. It seems that the Wall Street community has done a great job of telling us that we haven't saved enough, that we have invested well enough, or that we just don't deserve a good retirement because we haven't sent them enough money. "Just trust us!" says the Wall Street money machine; "of course you will be able to retire and stay retired. Have we ever let you down before?" Yes. Yes they have. If you had money in the financial markets (or owned a home) in 2001 or 2008, you know what it was like to be let down: years' worth of gains went away like puffs of smoke. Is this any way to run a retirement?

The Retirement Dilemma is this: *"Do I put my retirement money at risk or do I invest it at practically no return?"*

If you have managed to retire with a significant amount of money in your 401(k) let me, first of all, congratulate you. You have managed to do what many people have not: provide yourself the means to financial independence. I work with people like you, and I admire you because you have had to make some sacrifices along the way to reach this point. We are the first generation to be left to our own devices when it comes to saving for retirement, and the results of the great 401(k) experiment have been mixed, to say the least. The 401(k) account was never designed to replace pension plans; the fact that it became the only retirement funding vehicle for retirement should be categorized under "unintended consequences."

In 1978 a rather obscure congressional assistant, Richard Stanger, inserted a rather obscure 869 word passage into a revision of the tax code that was designed to allow high income employees a way to shelter some of their earnings. The passage is now known as the ubiquitous 401(k) retirement savings plan, and once corporate accountants realized that this was the golden ticket to rescue corporations from expensive fixed pensions, it became the most famous passage of the tax code known to man.

Corporations took billions of dollars of pension liabilities off their balance sheet and dumped it squarely on the shoulders of their workers. Today the baby boom generation is retiring at the rate of 10,000 people a day and largely hoping that their retirement savings will provide them with the means to retire and stay retired. Like an aerialist working without a net, we are left to perform an intricate task with no margin for error: if we fail to properly manage our finances we could be left with no retirement assets.

According to the Center for Retirement Research at Boston College, the median account balance of 401(k) and individual retirement accounts for households headed by people 55 to 64 years old was $120,000 in 2010. I should note that this is per household, not per individual person in the household—hardly enough to generate enough income to sustain a middle-class lifestyle in retirement. The 401(k), which like Social Security was designed to supplement retirement, has now become the primary source of retirement funding for an entire generation. We are the lab rats, and laissez-faire economics is our opponent. Here in 2015 we see almost daily media reports highlighting the ever increasing gap between wealthy Americans and poor Americans and many believe that do-it-yourself retirement investing is driving economic inequality. Left to their own devices, individual investors are often too aggressive or, more often, too conservative in their investment choices. By and large, they have often not saved enough during their working years for retirement, and during times of personal financial emergencies, they have often dipped into their retirement accounts.

Monique Morrissey and Natalie Sabadish, in a report titled "The Retirement Inequality Chart Book", for the Economic Policy Institute stated:

> The shift to a retirement system based on individual savings also means that workers' retirement prospects are increasingly affected by shocks to stock and housing markets and broader economic trends. Much of the 401(k) era coincided with a long bull market propping up household wealth measures even as traditional pensions became scarcer and the savings rate declined. This house of cards collapsed in 2001, and then again at the end of 2008.

I am sure that you know people, perhaps even family members, who have had to spend some (or all) of their retirement accounts to get themselves out of some kind of financial trouble. For every successful person I know who has saved for retirement I can name two who have not. With access to their retirement funds, Americans have borrowed or withdrawn money to pay for their kids educations, get through the financial crisis of 2001, or the aftershock in 2008. In fact, those of us who didn't touch our retirement money lost $2 trillion in the 15 months leading up to 2008, thanks to the stock market collapse, according to the Congressional Budget Office.

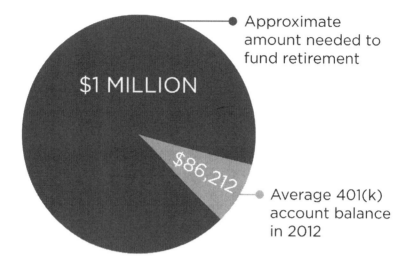

According to the Vanguard Group, in 2012 the average account balance in our 401(k) was $86,212, which is probably skewed by the larger accounts held by wealthier people. Many experts think that you need close to $1 million to fund your retirement, so the national retirement crisis (along with the student loan crisis) will be the subject of the media and legislation for years to come. In short, our generation's lab-rat-like experience as do-it-yourself retirement managers has largely failed. Is it any wonder that baby boomers are reluctant to retire and collect their last paycheck?

The Bins and Gaps Retirement Planning Process

After many years in the financial services industry, I began to realize that there is a logical and relatively simple way to decide if somebody has enough assets to retire. What began as my back of the envelope calculation turned into a useful series of formulas that help even the most unsophisticated investors to see their retirement possibilities: I call it "The Bins and Gaps Method of Retirement Planning." It's simple and comprehensible by anyone who has ever gone grocery shopping!

Remember when your mom used to send you to the grocery store to pick up a few things for her? She would write you a list, estimate how much money you would need, and send you off on your bike to the A&P (Okay, I got sent to the A&P, and in the sixties I would even have to buy her cigarettes). In financial planning terms this what your Mom did: she projected a budget and gave you enough money make sure it was funded.

Realistically; financial planning (and especially retirement planning) should be that simple. For all of the calculators, hypothetical illustrations, and computer-generated portfolios that Wall Street throws at you, it comes down to this: can you meet your monthly obligations? The Bins and Gaps Method helps you to identify your projected retirement assets and helps you to allocate your funds during your retirement. I'd like to suggest that you strive to keep your concept of retirement planning this simple: it's like going to the grocery store. Sure, it can be made a LOT more complicated, but you should always reduce the complexity down to this: have I funded my expenses?

Like any wonderful science experiment, retirement planning has some variables; in fact, it has more variables than constants! We don't know how many assets you have; we don't know what your monthly expenses are; we don't know what kind of rate of return you will earn on your assets, and we don't know how long you are going to live. Everything about your retirement is variable and completely dependent upon your decisions. But no matter how you fill in the numbers, retirement planning is simply a matter of knowing whether or not you have enough assets coming in to cover your expenses. It's that simple.

The first thing you can control is your monthly budget. My friends, at our lunch, developed a retirement budget that allowed them to cherish the important things in their lives, like family, while still living a relatively simple life. Before anyone retires I always suggest that they try a "practice retirement" where they live according to a projected retirement budget, an exercise that can be very enlightening. Do I advocate extreme austerity in retirement? Only if you are comfortable living frugally; rather, I am hoping that you come up with a comfortable and realistic number. We'll talk more about this later.

The next step is to decide if you have enough guaranteed income to cover your projected budget. We usually look at Social Security as one of our guaranteed sources of income, and I have devoted a chapter to maximizing your monthly SS income. Besides Social Security we look at any pension income you might have, other annuitized payments, or any other form of guaranteed lifetime income. If you have more income than expenses, like my friends, you have a "Funded" retirement and you can focus on planning for contingencies like the death of a spouse, saving for major events, and estate planning.

If your guaranteed income does not cover your anticipated expenses you are said to have a Gap. All we do now is multiply that monthly gap times 12 to get an Annual Gap and then times the number of years until you turn 100 to get your Lifetime Gap. (So a 65-year-old with a $500 monthly gap has a $6,000 annual Gap and a $210,000 Lifetime Gap.) If you have enough assets in your retirement account to pay your Lifetime Gap (In our example, more than $210,000), you also have a "Funded" retirement. Your job is to make sure that your retirement fund assets keep pace with inflation while you also focus on contingencies like death of a spouse, saving for major events, and estate planning. A "Funded Retirement" does not mean a "paid up" retirement, and if you increase your living expenses, suffer serious investment losses, or otherwise deviate from the plan, you could fall into the "Unfunded" category. This is tricky stuff, but not unmanageable.

If your mother sent you to the store without enough money to cover your shopping list; you were Unfunded. In the same way, if you don't have enough assets set aside in your retirement accounts, right now, to cover your Lifetime Gap, you have an Unfunded Retirement. Your ability to live the lifestyle that you want to lead is now at risk; you will either need extraordinary investment results, a part time job, or a winning lottery ticket to fill your retirement gap. It's your choice whether to try to adjust your budget downwards or try to generate more cash at this point, but at least we have defined the problem and can begin to plan for it. Perhaps you can defer retirement a while longer and spend a few years really focused on improving your retirement finances. We'll talk, at length, about these choices in a later chapter, but one way to reverse engineer your retirement planning is to simply divide the current balance of your assets by the number of years until you turn 100 to get an idea of how much of your gap you can fill each year.

THE BINS METHOD

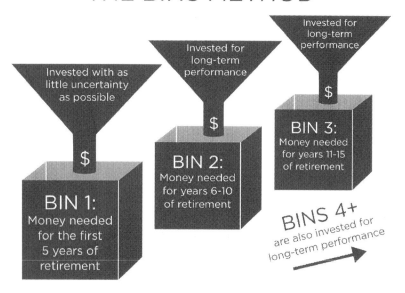

The final step in the Bins and Gaps Retirement Planning process is allocating your retirement assets to "Bins." A Bin is nothing more than a theoretical place to store investment dollars, and, in this case, we divide your assets based upon your years in retirement. Our theory is that the money you might need in the first five years of retirement is money that should be invested with as little uncertainty as possible, while the assets for your later years can be invested in asset classes that have traditionally done well over more meaningful periods of time albeit with more short term volatility. I love the idea of knowing that the assets designed to pay your immediate income in retirement are always invested in short term and fixed investments, removing your day to day spending money from the volatility of the financial markets.

As I've already mentioned, I'm willing to simplify things until they reach the easiest level at which they can be understood. I've borrowed a secret from professional money managers for this strategy. Instead of fixating on relative performance, some institutional investors such as many pension funds, use a metric known as "Funded Ratio." When applied to a your situation, this ratio is the sum of your current assets and retirement income streams (Social Security and any pensions) over your eventual retirement expenses, including taxes. If your assets and retirement income equal your expenses, your funded ratio is one. Less than one means you may be Unfunded, and more than one means you're in good shape, or Funded.

FUNDED RATIO

$$\frac{\text{Your retirement assets} + \text{Retirement income streams}}{\text{Eventual retirement expenses, including taxes}}$$

This may sound a bit technical, but at its core, it's quite simple: It shows what portion of your future total retirement expenses you're likely be able to pay, based on where you are now. The reason that pension funds use this measure is that they have to write checks to investors who are withdrawing their pension assets when they retire. So it's only logical for them to constantly monitor their status against this goal; so should you! Comparing your individual investment return to measures like the Dow Jones average or the S&P 500 is a nice number to know, but not necessarily all that useful; rather, you should simply strive to stay "Funded."

Flexibility

We're going to spend a lot of time talking about the current market conditions here in early 2015. But whether interest rates are at historic lows, as they are now, or if they go to historic highs sometime during your retirement, having a certain amount of flexibility in your investment portfolio is critical. One of the most important tenets of this book is that *you can't predict financial markets or interest rates with any certainty,* so it is better to design a portfolio that has the flexibility to react to changing economic conditions. If you know anything, we know that financial markets have a certain cyclicality. When the economy slows, the government lowers interest rates to stimulate, when the economy picks up the government raises interest rates to prevent inflation. Stocks tend to move in concert with interest rates while also playing their own tune; markets respond to everything from the business climate to bad storms. An old Wall Street guy once told me to think of a child with a yo-yo on an escalator. Focus on the escalator not the yo-yo. (This works on both up and down bound escalators!)

Assuming You Are Ready To Retire

We're going to talk a lot in this book about the choices you have when it comes to retirement investing. The choices you make as to how to invest your money are among the most important decisions you will ever make; right up there with choosing a mate, deciding where to send your kids to school, and who inherits your money. I came up with the title of this book, "The Retirement Dilemma," because at this point in history we have reached the perfect conditions to make investing potentially perilous. With interest rates at generational lows and the stock market at record high valuations; you could not create more difficult conditions to make important life changing investment decisions if you were a mad scientist in a lab. If you want to lock in interest rates right now at record lows, go right ahead, but think of how that will feel when you're 90 and a loaf of bread costs $75! Or go ahead and jump in the stock market and watch some of your money evaporate the next time we have a 2008-like stock market correction. It almost seems as though there are no good choices right now. A lot of advisors, colleagues of mine, are recommending fixed immediate annuities to their clients, trading principal for a lifetime of income that they cannot outlive. While this may seem like an expedient and safe method of managing retirement funds it also involves no small amount of risk. Choosing to live on a fixed income for the rest of your life, with no cost-of-living increases or money set aside for emergencies, comes with its own type of risks. It seems that any retirement choice we make, even the seemingly safest, is potentially dangerous.

Baby Boomers are the first generation to be held totally responsible for their own retirement in the modern age. Few of us have our parents' pension payments to depend on and, as Boomers, we have grown accustomed to a certain lifestyle that our depression-era parents only came to know as they reached maturity. We like gourmet food, fine wine and craft beer, and trips to Europe to discover both. We like having a couple of cars, a boat, and MasterCard bills. We are, at least so far, not that impressed with a simple lifestyle. We like to buy stuff. We love stuff. We like all of the modern conveniences, and our lifestyle reflects the fact that we are humans living in the digital age and we don't plan to lower our standard of living in retirement.

That being said, we plan to redefine retirement, and by redefine we mean that we will not retire until they drag us kicking and screaming from our jobs. Many boomers I know are afraid that they will not be able to stay retired once they leave work because of their lifestyle commitments. Going to live with our kids doesn't appear to be an option since they are already living with us! Our kids are loaded down with student loan debt, car payments, and health insurance premiums. They have not left the nest as globalization, and America's shrinking manufacturing base, have made it difficult for anyone to get a start in the world. Those of us who have jobs and good careers are very hesitant to leave them; especially with life expectancy being longer now than ever in history.

Since the late financial crises of 2001 and 2008, interest rates have been at generational lows, and the distinction between "savers" and "investors" has been entirely blurred. When I began in the financial services industry, over 30 years ago, the first thing I tried to do was determine if my prospective client was a saver or an investor. Savers were people who had enough money (or at least felt that they did) and they simply wanted to earn a decent return on their holdings without risking principle. In short, you either saved money to eventually spend it or to invest it. An investor was someone who was willing to put their money at risk and who sought a commensurate return for that risk. And, 30 years ago, there were a variety of investment vehicles available to savers, from certificates of deposit to zero coupon treasury bonds. Interest rates were high enough that savers could plan a retirement with a lump sum of money that paid high current interest rates with relative safety of principal. In fact, many retirees planed their entire retirement with no plans to ever touch principal, living simply off the interest and dividends from their investments.

Today, with interest rates so low, there is no reward for being a saver, in fact your savings might not be earning any interest at all, and I have been reading articles recently about the advent of "negative savings accounts," where the banks charge you a fee to hold your money! The world financial markets have been democratized, and the result is that a whole class of people who never would have considered becoming bondholders, shareholders, or even option traders are now checking their retirement plan balances daily and spending a lot of energy trying to outdo the professionals on Wall Street. The result is that the stock markets have "melted up": with no other place for money to go, equity prices have reached record highs. We have been forced to become a nation of speculators trying to stay one step ahead of the poor soul who is going to buy our shares when we sell them to him. The concept of becoming a shareholder of a company, of owning a share of a business that you plan to own for a long time, has been replaced by the individual investor who is trying to stay one step ahead of Wall Street. We have become market timers, amateur asset allocators, and amateur sideshow fortune-tellers. It is, as a friend of mine would call it, a tough hustle. Because so many of us have become accidental shareholders, the engineers and data collectors who make a living creating formulas and algorithms have conveniently created a one size fits all investment strategy just in time to lure us all in: The Index Investment. The very concept of index investing—that you will outperform other investors by investing exactly the same way as everyone else does—is fundamentally flawed.

Death by Data

The concept of being a long-term stock investor, one who understands a business, its competitors, and the value of the shares being purchased has been replaced by one size fits all investments. It has become common knowledge that everyone should own the same investment as almost everyone else. Investing, however, is often most successful when you are going against the tide. Everyone likes to think that they buy and low and sell high, but investing with the crowd makes that more difficult.

If you remember investing in the 1960's and 70's you'll no doubt remember the collection of "One Decision Stocks" called the "Nifty Fifty." It was said that if you built a portfolio of these stocks, you would not have to do any further research or any further diversification. It was so simple! Of course, as the popularity of Nifty Fifty investing spread, the value of the 50 stocks did indeed climb to record highs, until the last person got in the door and a bear market ensued. The Nifty Fifty under-performed broader market averages and became synonymous with the futility of formulaic investing. Today some of the stocks in the Nifty Fifty are still around while many are extinct, and we grizzled veterans of the stock market are skeptical of the delusions and madness of crowds, especially when the madness becomes "common knowledge."

Thanks to the digitalization of the world, we only believe things that can be quantified; we love data. And in no place is this more evident than in the investment world. Stock experts used to have "feet on the ground," meaning that they would actually speak to people who work in a certain industry, interview the key management players in a company, and use their judgment and experience to decide whether or not to buy shares in a certain stock or industry. Alas, feet on the ground, judgment, and experience are difficult to quantify; so we have come to rely on metrics like earnings-per-share, PE ratio, and Alpha to judge whether or not to invest in a company.

We measure the measurable, not necessarily the meaningful, and our entire investment selection process has come down to being able to read metrics. Even though all the investment literature we read tells us that "past results are not indicative of future performance," we still want to see data. We believe in science and the power of looking backwards. No place is this more evident than in the modern phenomenon of index investing. An index is a way to measure the performance of a group of stocks. More exactly, it measures the movements in a group of companies' stock prices—not how these companies take care of their clients, not what their future prospects are, not about any new innovations coming down the pike, not the quality of management, or anything else that might mean the company is not being run by idiots but by responsible, entrepreneurial grownups. No, an index simply measures the stock price of a company which, ultimately, is simply the measurement of the behavior of other stock buyers. An index tells us one thing: what the buyers and sellers before us did.

In the 1960's the Efficient Market Theory attained almost unanimous popularity; some academicians from Chicago told us that the only way you could possibly judge a company's value was by its stock price since all pertinent news about a company was out there and already reflected in the price of a stock. This theory led to a generation of corporate management who learned to manage for the short term to manipulate stock prices while they cashed in their personal stock options and sold the companies out from underneath the employees' feet (and wiped out their pension plan too!) The only thing was, Efficient Market Theory really didn't work. It was too easily manipulated, and these manipulations led to the short-term speculative attitude that now defines Wall Street.

To make the indexing process even more incestuous, the companies in an index are weighted so that the bigger companies count significantly more towards the value of an index, so the S&P 500, for example, is not an equal weighting of 500 companies. How do we determine what a bigger company is? By sales? By happy customers? By new patents? Nope, we measure the size of the company by the value of all of its shares (we call this capitalization). A company, therefore, with a million shares priced that day at $5 has a capitalization of $5 million. If the company's share price were to be cut in half, the company's capitalization would be too. Because Index Investing requires you to believe that all facts about the company are already somehow accounted for in the stock price (Efficient Market Theory) then the only relevant way to judge a company is by the current price of its shares. And since it is impossible to be more efficient than an efficient market there is no point in trying to outperform it. Investors need only passively purchase the index; so says current common knowledge.

By design, as I mentioned, the Indexes are weighted towards the bigger companies, so if you buy the S&P 500 Index, you are not actually buying an equal distribution of 500 stocks, but a portfolio of stocks that is heavily weighted towards the larger companies. (The S&P 500 is a capitalization weighted index of 500 stocks designed to measure performance of the broad domestic economy through changes in the aggregate market value of 500 stocks representing all major industries. Like all other indices, it is unmanaged and cannot be invested in directly.)

Now, if you grab your cell phone and open the calculator function, a little simple addition will show you how concentrated your portfolio actually is if you buy the "diversified" S&P 500. The top five stocks in the list above constitute 11.08% of your holdings. So when you consider the billions of dollars being invested in the various forms of investments in that "index," you realize that an awful lot of money is chasing these 5 stocks. If we add in the weighting of the next five stocks, our calculator tells us that 17.54% of our funds are invested in just 10 stocks. And further addition tells us that 31.387% of our assets are invested in the top 20 stocks of the S&P 500! By the time we get down to the less weighted stocks in the index, we are hardly getting a reasonable level of diversification; we have, essentially, a modified Nifty Fifty for the new millennium.

Savers, in today's world, are being turned into speculators, and Wall Street, with its inclination for mass marketing, has created a virtue cycle of investing that will continue to go up as long as people keep streaming in the door. What happens if they don't? In 2008, Baby Boomer investors watched in horror as their savings fell spectacularly and suddenly, mostly before they could react. For those already retired, incomes fell and portfolio values were reduced, in some cases permanently, as many investors sold their shares and refused to re-enter the markets in time for the eventual market recovery.

The lesson we should have learned in 2001 and again in 2008 is that capitalism is a dangerous sport and those of us who think that Wall Street is a money machine, or that there is no such thing as risk, are a tad too naïve to play with the big kids. At one time, during the second Bush administration, there was serious discussion about turning our Social Security accounts into personal, market based portfolios, an idea that mercifully disappeared after the events of 9/11 and the subsequent stock market crash.

Having a professionally selected and managed portfolio is a way to potentially build wealth, and over significant periods of time stocks have performed very well, but investors should always understand the risk they are assuming. There are no guarantees when it comes to investing, and one should be particularly careful about investing a retirement nest egg in the financial markets.

I like to think about it this way: I like a "deal." I'm a sucker for the buy-one-get-one-free bins at our local grocery store, I like to get a deal on a car when I buy one, and I sure don't like to overpay for anything, especially stocks. The very idea of buying a stock because everyone else already has bought it is an anathema to me. I just won't do it. My investment hero, Warren Buffet, puts it this way: "If I wanted to buy a farm I would first understand that about every 2 in 7 years there is a horrible drought, and I would wait until the depths of a drought and buy my farm then, when farms were selling for very distressed prices." In other words, Mr. Buffet likes to buy assets when they go on sale which, I humbly suggest, is the opposite of buying an Index Investment in 2015!

The problem, as I have said, with all forms of formulaic investing is that it is based on data that has already been accumulated; computers can't tell the future. And if you have some computer model that tells you to buy something that is obviously already fully valued, why would you override your common sense? And that's what investing should come down to: an interpretation of data rooted in common sense. If you can't explain why you are buying something in no more words than it takes to fill up a bumper sticker then you should not buy it. If you've been smart enough to accumulate a few assets, then you probably should trust your instincts.

What About Not Investing?

So if you don't want to buy bonds with interest rates so low, or stocks when they are at record highs, isn't it tempting to just let your money sit idly in a money market account? I mean, if we don't take any risk, we'll know that my money is available, at all times, right? And to some extent, you are right. You have short term needs; you'd be foolish to risk having your money in any investment that could drop in value overnight if you depended upon that money to cover your living expenses! (Back to common sense again, right?) And as we'll describe in later chapters, understanding risk is your responsibility as an investor; even if you hire a professional advisor, he should be making you aware of the risks that he wants you to assume.

What, then, is the risk of playing it very, very safe? Well, for one thing, you may be spending principal. Cash is subject to a loss of purchasing power over time, for another. Finally, interest rates are so low right now that it is awfully scary to see your money doing nothing. Cash, I would suggest, has a place in every portfolio. And depending upon your income needs, a percentage of your retirement money in an emergency fund and in a fund for current expenses is not only recommended, but wise indeed. However, a sustainable retirement plan should include assets that seek to provide Income, Growth of Income, and Growth. I'll talk more about this Triad approach to funding your retirement in later chapters, but for now, let's just say that cash is not the only tool professionals use in planning a lifetime of retirement income.

You at One Hundred

The concept of retirement came about when you weren't expected to live more than a few years after you retired. Today we can reasonably expect to live 20 to 40 years after we collect our last paycheck, so our retirement plan needs to reflect a lifetime of income. And not only should our income be consistent and dependable, it should also have the ability to increase over time. If you, for example, locked all of your assets into a fixed investment that you can't outlive, twenty years from now, the effects of inflation on your purchasing power might leave you wishing you had the ability to increase your income as you get further into retirement.

As self-appointed pension planners, we not only have to figure out how to get an immediate income, we must also try to anticipate our future income needs and the effects of inflation on our purchasing power. Did you pay less for your first house than for your last car? I did. Inflation is a fact of life, and even though we are not measuring any significant inflation in our economy in the last few years, you can be assured that during your retirement some costs of living will increase. Living a longer, happier retirement means that maintaining your spending power is something you should plan for.

The Roof Blew Off!

Here's something else to consider: unexpected major expenses. If, hypothetically, you had $500,000 in a retirement account and you were somehow able to magically get an 8% guaranteed rate of return (I don't think you can right now, this is just a number I picked to illustrate a point), and you were comfortably living on your Social Security and the $40,000 a year from your retirement account, all might be going well until you hit a bump in the road. Let's say a storm blows your roof off. In our example, you would either have to finance the payments for the roof (and interest) out of current cash flow, or you would have to deplete your funds that are paying you a monthly income, killing at least a part of the goose that is laying the monthly income egg. Once you spend some of your income-producing funds, your income is probably reduced for life.

A perfectly funded retirement plan has assets set aside to take care of unexpected and major events. These funds are not designated for generating income or for every day expenses, rather, they are set aside for things like new roofs. Or world cruises. Or new cars. (Or, in my case, new road bikes. The number of bicycles I want to own is best described by the formula "N + 1" where N represents the number of bicycles I already own.)

A Rigid State of Flexibility

There is hope; The Bins and Gaps method of retirement planning is designed to provide current income while anticipating your future income needs. One of the benefits of the self-funded retirement over the old fashioned pension plan is that a properly designed retirement portfolio can react to changes in both your life and in the economy. The key to retaining flexibility is to diversify and begin to view your retirement years in Five Year Bins (I'm going to talk about this a lot more in a later chapter). In the meantime, let's just know that your life, and the financial landscape that helps define it, will change. Just as your interests and ability to travel might change as you go further into retirement, so might the interest rates that determine whether you are a saver or investor. While it would be foolish to lock all of your funds into interest bearing instruments (like bonds) for the next thirty years with interest rates at their current lows, it would be equally foolish to speculate with all of your money.

A properly designed plan should allow you to account for rising and falling interest rates, volatile financial markets, and changes in your lifestyle. For example, a couple might be enjoying two Social Security checks until one of them passes way, then the survivor is left with only one check. A properly designed plan should have the flexibility to increase income payments to make up for the lost SS benefits. Or interest rates, at some point during retirement, might rise to the level of the 1980's and our retirees might find that they have a perfect opportunity to move some of their assets to federally insured certificates of deposit. This type of flexibility should not require active trading or over managing accounts, rather, annual reviews and keeping a reasonable amount of flexibility in the account should be all that is required.

Sounds Easy, Right?

So have I described some of the issues you've been facing lately as you think about retiring? I hope I have and maybe even mentioned a few more. Because deciding whether or not to retire is among a handful of the most important decisions you are liable to ever make, and the current conditions of the financial markets have not made deciding any easier. The funny thing about managing money is that the rules of the game are always changing. Just when we think we can live off interest income and never invade principal, the rules change, and interest rates go almost all the way to zero. When we think it's safe to invest in stock, an event like 9/11 comes along and wipes out years of gains. Planning for retirement is not something that the average retiree should attempt at home, even if he does have lightning fast wireless and a subscription to CNBC.

Let's go a little more in depth into what your retirement should look like and how you can think about Minding Your Gaps and Filling Your Bins.

3

DECIDING IF YOU ARE
READY TO RETIRE

**Tell me you want the kind of things
that money just can't buy.
Lennon and McCartney**

I'm really excited to be writing this chapter for you, I'm sure that you are approaching your retirement decision with equal measures of trepidation and some excitement, so let me give you a couple of hints that will help you be comfortable. In this chapter, I am going to give you some tips that I have picked up by working with people getting ready to retire throughout my career. I often speak to retirement groups about finances and I've come to the conclusion that when it comes to retirement, money isn't everything. So, before we get to the financial aspects of retirement, let me ask you, what is the key to a successful retirement? For me, it can be summed up in one word: Engagement.

Engagement: That feeling you get when you first wake up in the morning and can't wait to get on with your day. At least for me; being engaged in life is what makes it worth living and I can't imagine heading into retirement without a plan to help me stay excited and interested in what life has for me. While this is a book about the financial aspects of retirement, let's talk about the emotional part for a few minutes; we'll get to the financial stuff soon enough.

My experience has been that people who retire without something meaningful in their lives go quietly crazy. In fact, it is my opinion that people often delay retirement for two reasons: they don't have a satisfactory financial plan, and they don't have a life plan. The two go hand in hand, and unless you find some sort of meaning in life, I believe that your retirement will be empty, lonely, or just plain old boring. Most of us can only play so much golf, fish just so much, or clean our house just so many times; staying vital, feeling needed, and being useful are as important as being able to afford nice things. Having money and the resources to retire is only half the equation, an important half, but not the entire answer to happiness. In a quote often attributed to Mark Twain it is said, although not strictly about retirement, "I've been rich and I've been poor. Rich is better." I don't know if this saying is necessarily universal; as a retirement planning expert I can tell you that I know many people with only modest assets who live meaningful and loving lives while I know many other poor souls who are wealthy but only can manage to watch the news all day and only venture out to go to the doctors. The difference: a passion for living.

I have a website and a Facebook page called "Middle Aged Crazy," and I am the proud leader of a tribe of mid-lifers who have allowed themselves to pursue their passions after they've raised their kids and launched their careers. My last book was called "When Do I Get To Be Me?" and it is about finding your passion for life by releasing your inner Creative Beast. In my case I have launched a plethora of new pursuits, often with my wife Teresa, like ballroom dancing, cooking school in Italy, learning guitar, becoming a long distance road cyclist, writing books, and even learning a foreign language. I went back to college in my fifties and finished my degree after taking a 35-year semester break. So, I know something about staying involved and passionate in life, and I tell you this because I have come to appreciate how short life can be and how precious our experience here can be. I hope that your retirement is exciting and stimulating; why would you choose any other way?

Not long ago I attended a memorial celebration for a fellow road cyclist who had passed away young, much too young, and I came away inspired to love just a little harder, to pedal just a little faster, and to continue to stay curious and passionate about my life. Even though I knew he was a successful business owner, no one talked about his professional accomplishments at his service. No, they remembered his sense of humor, his strength, and how much he loved his family. Money wasn't mentioned, even once, at this celebration of his life, and judging from the wide variety of people at his service, he didn't make having money a criteria for being his friend. My lesson, which I want to share with you, is that money is a nice piece of the puzzle, but not the only piece. I hope, as you prepare for retirement, that you are prepared to really continue living!

You Can Practice Retirement

Have you ever been in a play or any other type of performance? How about on a team? Can you imagine taking the stage or the field without rehearsal or practice? I have to tell you something: I was a member of a comedic improv troupe and even something as spontaneous as improv is pretty well rehearsed. We practiced being open to ideas, listening skills, finding the joke in most any scene, and most importantly, learning to trust one another. So when we ask the audience for suggestions like, "Give me a place you worked, and a type of meal to prepare," we haven't rehearsed the actual scene we are about to create, but we have practiced the framework for just about any situation that might come up on stage. Preparation is important to just about any human endeavor, so why on earth wouldn't you want to prepare for your retirement?

When I teach a class on retirement planning I am sure to spend some time on planning to practice your retirement. I ask my students to visualize their typical week in retirement, what will their life look like once they don't have to report to work? Will they golf every day? Will they move to a retirement community? For someone who is going to volunteer, I ask them to spend some time in the organization now, for someone who wants to fish every day, I suggest that they find some friends who can take them out to fish. In fact, the whole, "try it before you buy it," concept is never more important than in preparing to retire.

If you are planning to move to Florida, or some other sunny climate when you retire, rent first! Take a few vacations and use Air B&B, a website where you can rent apartments and homes all over the world, to see if you actually fit into the community in which you are thinking about retiring. As is the case with my financial recommendations, I value flexibility and the ability to change your mind during retirement. There would be nothing worse than moving to a new community because it sounds like a nice place to retire only to find that you don't really like it there and that you are stuck with a house that you can't sell.

One of the more common complaints that I've heard about from new retirees is that sudden "forced togetherness" of couples who have each lived happy lives with their own identities, who retire and are now together ALL THE TIME. You know, she is used to doing the grocery shopping by herself, suddenly she is joined by HIM, the retired Type A executive who now wants to manage the grocery shopping instead of his department. (Here in Florida I see this type of couple in the grocery store all the time; I have to try not to laugh out loud when he pulls out the calculator with the big buttons and she wants to pummel him with the laundry detergent he decided was the best buy!) Or she decides to take up golf and wants to join her low handicap spouse on the links every morning—not the relaxing retirement that he envisioned at all! Practice makes perfect, or at least it shows us what we need to avoid!

The Anticipated Retirement Budget

So as long as you are practicing retirement, it is crucial that you begin the keep track of ALL of your anticipated expenditures in retirement. The Anticipated Retirement Budget (ARB) is one of the keys to proper retirement planning, and I cannot express how crucial it is to have an idea as to how your money is going to be spent in the days and years after you have collected your final paycheck. In fact, the rest of the retirement planning methods in this book are based upon this important figure, the more accurate your ARB is, the more likely you are to make a good decision about the timing of your retirement.

My approach to retirement planning is a little different than most of the Wall Street advice you are likely to encounter, since most financial advice seems to be designed into scaring or shaming you into saving more money. My approach is a little more practical; at this point in your life it is probably too late to save a significantly larger amount of money than you have already saved, so there is no point in beating yourself up or working until the day you die. My approach is much more pragmatic: *let's figure out how much money you need to live in retirement and whether you have enough assets to support that lifestyle.* That's all; it's not rocket science. Sure, you may need to defer retirement a few years, or you may need to lower your anticipated standard of living, but we won't know until you come up with your own unique and very personal ARB, and then we let the numbers tell us if we can achieve our retirement goal or not. You might be surprised; when you take into account your Social Security income and any other pension income, you might be perfectly fine. In truth, we won't know until you come up with that number: your ARB.

I don't care if you have $20 million or $20 thousand in your retirement account; if you don't have a fairly accurate Anticipated Retirement Budget you are wasting your time trying to plan for retirement (although it would be more fun to waste time with the $20 million dollar account.) The basis for all retirement planning, quite simply, is this:

"Do I have enough assets to support my lifestyle for the rest of my life?"

For all of the spreadsheets, questionnaires, and algorithms that we financial guys throw at you, you should just want to get to the bottom line: can you pay your bills? The basis for the financial side of retirement planning is no more complicated than answering this question: have you selected a lifestyle that you can afford? All of this assumes that you are retiring voluntarily, that you have had time to plan your retirement lifestyle, and that you retain some control as to whether you continue to work or not. If you are retired, but not by choice, I understand, and I don't mean to talk over you, you already have made some hard choices in your life regarding your lifestyle or by looking for a job.

As you begin to look at your projected retirement budget I hope you can see the wisdom in doing a practice retirement first! By envisioning every aspect of your retirement ahead of time, and even rehearsing it, you will get a real feel for the items that need to be included in your budget, and those that don't. If this process scares you, or even seems impossible, I urge you to give it a shot anyway; you might find that once you get past your initial resistance to budgeting that you might actually find yourself getting excited about the next chapter in life!

The Television Commercial Version of Retirement

They come at us whenever we are watching shows that are, shall we say, age appropriate. CBS Sunday Morning, PGA Golf, and re-runs of Matlock. In between the commercials for adult diapers, mesothelioma lawsuits, and dating sites for old people come the ads from the giant Wall Street firms, banks, and insurance companies. You've always wanted a vineyard, or to sail around the world, or to take all 12 of your grandkids to Epcot at once, haven't you? Yup, all you have to do is go see your local bank teller, and it is a fait accompli; you and your affluence will live happily ever after. The only question is whether you want your vineyard to be in Napa or Tuscany. Don't you hate such difficult choices?

Some of us are lucky enough to be able choose the date we will collect our last paycheck. Others... well not so much. Whether they call it downsizing, corporate restructuring, or our company closing around us, some of us find ourselves in involuntary retirement. Either way; living a retirement life-style requires a different mindset than when we are working, and hopefully we have some, if not all, of the resources we need to have a fulfilling second act to our lives. For some of us, keeping a part time job is the only alternative, for others it is not. So how do you decide if you have the financial assets to live like those people in the stock brokerage commercials?

This is, after all, a book about finance and I'd like to call a timeout right here and say something that is considered blasphemous on Wall Street: plenty of people have figured out that money doesn't equal happiness, and it is highly likely that you can find peace in retirement even if your only source of income is Social Security. I'm sure you know people who live simple, low cost lives and who consider themselves happy, engaged, and fulfilled. In fact, I know many people who have plenty of assets who manage to get by without a chauffeur and a Rolls. A large part of retirement is about slowing down, lowering the pressure on yourself and easing up on the consumerism. I'm pretty sure that you will never feel ready to retire until you make that shift.

Retirement, after all, isn't for everybody. In my case, for example, I can't imagine not having something to do every day and not having a business to run. Servant leadership, my management philosophy, means that I come to work with the attitude of "who can I help today?" and I am lucky enough to have found a career that is mentally challenging with almost no physical component, I am not exactly wearing myself out when I am analyzing a retirement cash flow report. Can I see myself working less? Absolutely, and as I get older having financial independence will give me the ability to choose when and where I work. And if health issues shall arise, money will give me some choices that I might not otherwise have.

Choices: that's what it's all about, isn't it? Having the option to travel is just about as important as traveling itself, we like to know we are pulling weeds in our garden because we want to be, not because we don't have any other options. For all my years as a financial planner, I haven't met a lot of people who live like the people in those commercials: a life of unrestrained consumerism. Just about every retired couple that I have worked with understand that resources are limited and that no small amount of stewardship is required to live life without any more paychecks.

Here's the thing I want you to recognize about those commercials, they are aimed at your emotions. In stock broker school, back in the 1980's, we were taught that you can only get people to invest money if you appeal to either the emotion of fear or that of greed. I've tried to reject this cynical approach to running a business but it is prevalent in my industry. From the imposing wood paneled office of the local brokerage office to the power tie your advisor wears, Wall Street sets out to intimidate you, to tell you that "while you may have a few bucks, you are not our biggest client, by far," and "we know more about money than you," and "if you don't hire us you will be making a very big mistake; after all, we have wood paneling and a fancy address."

And while you should be fearful of running out of money, and traveling the world in luxury sounds nice to everyone, I'd like to suggest a simpler, more scientific model of deciding when you are ready to go in for your last day. Let's try something radical: design your own retirement lifestyle and create a personal budget!

Because I've been working with folks ready to retire for so long, I've developed a couple of dispassionate and simple formulas that give me a quick snapshot into someone's ability to retire successfully, and I'm going to reveal them to you in an upcoming chapter. Before we can apply these formulas, we'll need a pretty accurate accounting of how much money you will need every month in retirement. I can't give you the numbers, and unless you're willing to go find out what they are, I believe that you shouldn't retire. Getting a grasp on your retirement budget is one of the most important things you can do as you prepare for retirement.

When it comes to money, emotions are not all that useful. Feelings are great, they are the window to your soul... I know, I get it. But when it comes to math: emotions are not required (or even useful). Positive thinking, expecting the best, and even using the magic of The Secret are all useless when it comes to deciding if you have the ability to retire or not. It comes down to a simple (if not painful) look at cash flow and the more preparation have done for retirement, the better the numbers will look.

The Practice Retirement Budget:

Remember the movie *Apollo 13* when the astronauts had to account for the weight of everything in the endangered space capsule to plan their re-entry to earth? (Okay, if you haven't seen the movie, let me ask you something: where have you been? Hasn't everyone seen *Apollo 13* by now?) Only after careful inventory and analysis did they realize that their calculations were off because the original flight plan had accounted for the weight of moon rocks; engineers and scientists had to make an adjustment based on current circumstances. I'm going to suggest that you need to do as comprehensive a set of plans as the rocket scientists at NASA. More than simply visualizing yourself in retirement, I want you to account for every dollar that you will spend in retirement before you get to the fun (and discretionary) stuff. As much as you are going to hate this, getting a handle on where your money is going is one of the most important things you are ever going to do.

Your Nut

I have a friend who retired from the circus; she worked in the real circus, the big top. She told me that when traveling circuses used to arrive in town the chief of police would take their lug nuts off of the wagons and hold onto them until the circus raised enough money to pay the tax for their engagement. So the phrase, "What's your nut?" became shorthand for your living expenses. And if you don't know this number there is a very good chance that your spouse, life partner, or significant other does. They are probably sitting in your recliner, watching a movie; go ask them. It's the first back of the envelope calculation you do when you're thinking about retiring.

As I said, knowing the total of your monthly expenses is the most important calculation you are likely to need. Let's face it, none of us would choose to retire if we knew that we couldn't eat, or pay rent, or buy gas. Let's talk a little bit about this calculation and some of the adjustments you can make as you prepare to collect your last paycheck ever. Have you done a retirement budget? Have you practiced?

Before you can make good decisions about retirement, I am pretty sure it would be a good idea to know what your current monthly living expenses are. Your next step will be to go through your list and see what stays and what goes during retirement. For example, you won't be making con-tributions to your retirement plan anymore, will you? And, the money you spend on commuting and lunches out every day? Expenses for a work wardrobe? Most of my clients are surprised at how much of their income is reinvested in work related expenses yet they find that there are new expenses associated with living the retirement lifestyle.

Many serious retirement planning experts suggest that you can retire on 70% of the income you had when working; but I'm not one of them. My experience has been, at least in the first several years of retirement (while you are young and healthy), that you spend as just about as much, if not more, than you spent when you were working. Like most personal finance concepts, formulas and rules of thumb are great guidelines, but your retirement experience is unique and personal. No one can do your retirement budget but you.

While very few of us have the discipline to live to a strict budget, my experience is that there is a certain amount of discipline required to enjoy a successful retirement, and before you retire I suggest that you compare your anticipated retirement spending with your anticipated retirement income.

I Owe, I Owe, So Off To Work I... Doh!

I am more than guilty of incurring debt; I am perhaps the poster child for buy now, pay later. I am this despite the fact that my grandparents, who lived through the Great Depression, warned me that incurring debt was the express lane to hell. If you can't pay for something in cash you just shouldn't buy it. Yet I still buy cars, vacations, and dinners on my credit card. How about you? Are you debt free? Let's talk about debt in regards to preparing for retirement.

Among families headed by those 55 or older, 65.4 percent are still carrying debt loads, according to the Washington, D.C.-based Employee Benefit Research Institute (EBRI). That is an increase of more than 10 percent from 1992, when only 53.8 percent of such families grappled with debt. And 9.2 percent of families headed by older Americans are paying at least 40 percent of their income to debt payments, up from 8.5 percent three years earlier. The reason: rising home prices and the longer-term mortgages that result, often leaving seniors with a high monthly nut well into their golden years. Seniors are also dealing with student debt; 706,000 senior households grappled with a record $18.2 billion in student loans in 2013, according to the U.S. Government Accountability Office.

DEBT AMONG FAMILIES HEADED BY THOSE 55 YEARS OR OLDER

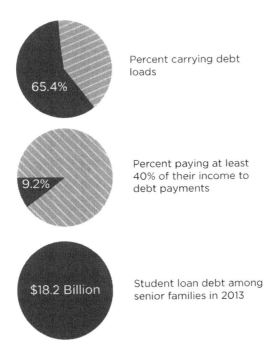

65.4%

Percent carrying debt loads

9.2%

Percent paying at least 40% of their income to debt payments

$18.2 Billion

Student loan debt among senior families in 2013

In my opinion, it is difficult to live a successful retirement if you are still paying for stuff you bought years ago. The cycle of debt, if you aren't careful, will continue after you have received your last paycheck; it stands to reason that if much of your cash flow is going towards debt repayment you will be tempted to borrow more to meet living expenses. So; what is the remedy? Is it good practice to liquidate retirement assets to pay off debt? Let's talk about it.

First off, I don't think having a reasonable mortgage is a bad idea. Paying a mortgage has some tax advantages, which may or may not benefit you, based upon tax bracket, and, at very least, you are building equity in your home as you go deeper into retirement. One of the advantages of today's economic environment is that mortgage rates are at extremely low levels. Not long ago a client of mine refinanced a thirty-year mortgage and was able to obtain a fifteen-year mortgage that actually had a lower monthly payment than he had before. In my client's case, he was able to refinance when he was 50 years old, meaning that his mortgage would be paid off at 65, a very nice retirement gift for himself!

The financial crisis of 2008 came about as a direct result of people borrowing against their home equity and then abandoning their homes and mortgages as home prices collapsed. For that reason, I urge anyone who is thinking of mortgaging their home, or even using a line of credit, to remember that the danger of defaulting on such a loan might cause you to lose your house, a risk that most of us would prefer to avoid at any time, but especially in retirement. Debt consolidation, in the form of a home equity loan, should only be considered if you have few other choices and if you are certain that your retirement budget has the income to cover the additional payments that come along with a refinancing.

So what about other debt? Credit cards, car payments, and so on? In general, I'd like to see this type of consumer debt paid off before you actually retire. Unsecured consumer debt like credit cards can have ridiculously high interest rates, often as high as 20%, and it is almost impossible to imagine that your investment portfolio can grow fast enough to outpace the rate of compound interest that the credit card companies are earning from you. But remember: as funds are withdrawn from your retirement accounts, they are taxed as ordinary income. And as your income increases, so does your tax rate. In addition, once you use the funds in your retirement account they are gone forever, they are no longer available to generate an income to supplement your retirement. Not only that, but if you are under 59 ½ years old, your withdrawals from your retirement accounts may be subject to a 10% penalty. So, for sure, avoid withdrawing from your retirement accounts until you have passed that age, but even then, cashing in your retirement accounts to pay off credit cards is not my favorite option. I'll recommend it if we don't have any other choices, but in general I'd like to use already taxed money to pay off this type of debt. So... what should you do?

Ideally, I'd like to see you pay off your credit cards before you retire, even if it means deferring retirement. Your after-tax dollars, the ones that come to you in your paycheck, are almost always the best dollars to pay off existing consumer debt. If you have savings in an investment account, a bank, or even a Roth IRA, I'd suggest drawing from these accounts to pay down consumer debt. Unless you get extremely lucky, it is unlikely that your investments or saving will earn a higher return than the one you are being charged by the credit card company. There's a reason, after all, that the banks have the skyscrapers and you don't.

If you don't have the assets to pay off your debt, I would urge you to establish an aggressive debt repayment plan and attempt to pay off everything that you owe as soon as possible, even if that payment plan takes the first few years of retirement. If you must use your retirement assets to pay down consumer debt, do so with some expert tax guidance. Debt consolidation loans are a reasonable consideration but I would avoid using my home to secure previously unsecured debt unless I was positive that I had the assets to make the monthly payments. Stretching out consumer debt payments over the life of a mortgage is, at best, a band aid, and at worst, a way to enrich bankers. Speaking of enriching bankers:

You Are Not a Bank

Let's file this one under Clear and Present Dangers: people who know you have done a good job of saving for your retirement may begin to view you as a "source of funds." I don't care how much your kids need money, how much your grandchildren need a new car, or if your brother has a great investment idea: you can't do it unless you can fill these needs from current cash flow. I see it happen all the time; it is quite a temptation to help out family, especially your grandkids, but if you use your retirement funds for something other than retirement, I hope that you have included some extra funds in your Projected Retirement Budget, otherwise you are going to deplete your lifetime funds. I have a friend, a long-time client, who was relating a story about his daughter to me and how she was tired of her job, and he was going to help her open up a restaurant. But keep in mind, I know this man, I love him and I know exactly how much money he has. And I can assure you that he did not have the money to open a pizza joint, especially since he is retired! We had a long and not unpleasant conversation about what his retirement would look like if he went into the restaurant finance business. He thanks me for being the voice of reason every time we talk.

The way the world works is that people who don't have any money probably don't understand what it is like to have money. They tend to think that people who do have money, especially retired family members, are a great source of capital. The fact is that the money you have set aside to fund your retirement has to last you a very long time (maybe 40 years?) And you cannot deplete principal simply because somebody thinks you have deep pockets. It's very tempting, even for ourselves, to want to solve everybody's problems because we have a monthly brokerage statement delivered to our house that displays a relatively large balance. I know you know this; I know I risk alienating you by mentioning this, but I've seen it happen a lot! Grandmothers are an especially soft touch; I know because my kids are always trying to get money out of their grandmothers, and you have to set the rules early and often that you are not an alternative source of funding for their needs. If a big bank won't loan them money, why in the world should you?

I believe that if you can give gifts or help your family out you should, provided it comes from current cash flow that is in excess or from assets that are not part of your retirement plan. Frankly, I'm in favor of you spending all of your money on yourself and living an actuarially perfect life; running out of money on the day you die. But since that's awfully hard to calculate, let's just assume that your family can spend all of your money after you're dead and gone; in the meantime let's be good stewards and make sure that we take care of ourselves first. It would be a shame to have to go live with your kids because you funded a pizza parlor that failed.

There, I'm glad we had that talk!

Sitting down and doing a practice retirement budget is not only frightening, it's boring. I understand. But let's face it: it has to be done and it's better to approach retirement with your eyes open than to discover that you have to go get a job and start all over again somewhere after you've retired from the place you worked for a long time.

So, here we are, you've paid off your consumer debt, you have a handle on your retirement expenses and now you need to generate an income. Let's start with the government and your Social Security retirement income.

4

MAXIMIZING SOCIAL SECURITY

**If you try sometimes, you just might find,
you get what you need.
The Rolling Stones**

As we design a retirement plan, Social Security is the first place we look to for income (that is, if you qualify; some people never paid into the system, and others paid into another type of government pension system). The first step to answering the question of whether you can retire or not begins with Social Security. That irritating Social Security withholding tax you've been paying for your entire career is now about to pay off. While we all have legitimate concerns as to whether Social Security will be there for us in the future, there can be no denying that it is available to us now and while the politicians argue over the future of Social Security, I believe that our best choice is to make plans based on the system as it stands now. For most people, Social Security benefits will not provide enough income to fully support them during retirement, but, nonetheless, deciding when to collect benefits and figuring out how to maximize them is an undeniably crucial first step to retirement planning. While it has become something of a cliché to matter-of-factly dismiss Social Security; we always say things like "Social Security, if it will still be there." The fact is that if you collect

$2000 a month in benefits and live over 30 years in retirement, you will collect well over $700,000 over the course of your lifetime. I don't know about you, but that amount of money still gets my attention. In addition, Social Security pays an annually increasing benefit thanks to its cost-of-living adjustment riders.

Social Security is a 75-year-old program designed to help senior citizens escape poverty in their old age. Although many of us tend to think of Social Security as a safety net, we should remember that it is a vital and important part of our retirement plan. And yes, the media likes to scream about the possibility of Social Security going broke, but in reality the system is currently paying claims and will continue to do so with no changes until the 2030s. I'll talk more in a minute about what will happen then, but in the meantime it would be irresponsible to do any retirement planning without taking into account the benefits that will be available to you. First we have to talk a little bit about what Social Security is, the common terms that come up when discussing your benefits, and strategies that can be employed to get the biggest return that you can.

First off let me say this: if you have no choice but to collect Social Security as soon as possible because you have no other sources of income, that's pretty much what you have to do. In a lot of the strategies we're going to talk about in this chapter, will be talking about deferring Social Security benefits until you're 70 years old, but you can start collecting when you reach 62 years old. And while delaying the collection of your SS income might be a perfectly acceptable strategy to someone who is either still working or has other retirement income, if you find yourself without a job and without sufficient assets to provide an income for you, collecting Social Security before you reach Full Retirement Age might be your only option. Social Security is, after all, a safety net, and many people are approaching retirement with no other source of income. If, however, you find yourself in a somewhat healthier financial position, or if you plan to keep working in your sixties, some of the strategies we will talk about in this chapter may be of great benefit to you.

As we create a financial plan for retirement, it is easy to take for granted the benefits of Social Security, but in reality it's a very unique and important retirement planning tool. Developed in 1935 to help rescue Americans from the Great Depression, SS is a payroll tax insurance program that you have bought and paid for. Because it has so many benefit options, many people can become confused as to the best ways to collect their monthly check. First off, Social Security has a predetermined amount of income that is based upon your earnings history and then applied to a formula the amount of income you've earned over your lifetime (or your spouse's). During your retirement you will receive a steady income that is highly unlikely to be cut at any time you are taking benefits. This income is for life; so some of the decisions that you make before collecting benefits will matter for many years. Thanks to cost-of-living adjustments Social Security benefits are usually raised every year. And there are survivor benefits built into the system that are specially designed to take care of widowed spouses.

Let's talk a little bit about some of the more important terms that you'll need to know when you begin to look into your Social Security options:

1) Primary Insurance Amount (PIA): this is an amount that you will receive each month. It is based on your 35 highest years of earnings. Note that this figure is based on your highest 35 years so if you worked 40 or 50 years only your highest years are included. These years are applied to a formula based upon your year of birth, and then they are indexed

for inflation. (I'm not going to get into the full formula here, but if you go to SocialSecurity.gov you'll find calculators and all kinds of useful tools.) You collect your entire primary insurance amount when you reach Full Retirement Age.

2) Full Retirement Age (FRA): the table below shows the year and month in which you will receive your full retirement benefits (PIA). Full retirement age for people born between 1943 and 1954 is 66 years old. As part of a congressional effort to save Social Security and as a nod to longer life expectancies, full retirement age begins to be delayed by several months based on the year the person claiming was born:

Benefit reduction for claiming benefits at age 62 under current law, by year of attaining age 62 and year of birth

Year of attaining age 62	Year of birth	EEA	FRA
1999 or earlier	1937 or earlier	62	65
2000	1938	62	65 and 2 months
2001	1939	62	65 and 4 months
2002	1940	62	65 and 6 months
2003	1941	62	65 and 8 months
2004	1942	62	65 and 10 months
2005–2016	1943–1954	62	66
2017	1955	62	66 and 2 months
2018	1956	62	66 and 4 months
2019	1957	62	66 and 6 months
2020	1958	62	66 and 8 months
2021	1959	62	66 and 10 months
2022 or later	1960 or later	62	67

Source: Social Security full retirement-age chart, available at http://www.socialsecurity.gov/retire2/agereduction.htm.

So in my case, since I was born in 1956, I will not be eligible to receive my Full Retirement Amount (FRA) until I am 66 years and four months old. It's important to note that I can still collect benefits when I am 66 years old; in fact I'll be able to claim them when I'm 62 years old, but I will not get my full retirement amount unless I apply for payments when I am 66 years and four months old. It's been my experience that once you start talking about Social Security that it is very easy to get confused when we start tossing around terms like FRA and PIA. So I'd like to suggest that you take a minute and write them down in the margin of the book or on a piece of paper. Even after years of financial planning, I still find myself getting lost sometimes in the government jargon that defines the Social Security system.

When Should You Collect?

The amount of money you collect every month from Social Security is based upon your age and your corresponding life expectancy. If you wait until your full retirement age to begin to collect you will receive more money per month than if you decided to collect at age 62. Going back to my age as an example, I will have the option to collect Social Security when I am 62 years old, but because I am four years and four months younger than I would be at full retirement age, I will collect a smaller benefit. Now wouldn't it be nice if I could start collecting at 62 and then get me Primary Insurance Amount when I reached Full Retirement Age? Yes, it would be great, but that's not how it works! The important thing to know is that once you make your selection it is pretty much set in stone (there are some exceptions that go beyond the scope of this book, but I do discuss them with my clients when we do a comprehensive retirement plan.) So if you decide to begin collecting Social Security at your first opportunity, at age 62, you have made a decision that will result in a lower monthly benefit for the rest of your life.

Here something else: if you delay collecting your Social Security until you are 70 years old, you will get an increased monthly benefit, one that is even higher than your Primary Insurance Amount, for the rest of your days. As I said, when I run into a client who has no other assets or sources of income, claiming Social Security benefits at age 62 is often the only option we have. But when someone is retiring a little later in life, or doesn't need an immediate income from Social Security, we will often consider delaying Social Security benefits. So this is the decision you have to make: do I want to start collecting benefits at age 62 at what will be a smaller amount, or do I want to defer until I am older? There are many factors involved in this decision including taxation, the work status of your spouse, and your overall health.

Keep in mind that life expectancy is still around 80 years old (it was 61 years old in 1935, when Social Security was created.) So your decision involves your ability to tell the future, more specifically, your ability to know the date you'll die. Since most of us are not privy to this information, we have to do what all mortals must do when considering such important matters: we make a really good guess. Here's a number that you might want to know: if you begin to collect Social Security benefits at age 62 your benefit will equal 75% of your Primary Insurance Amount. So if your primary insurance amount is $2466, and you decide to collect at age 62, your benefit would be $1849.50. Now for fun, let's assume that your Full Retirement Age is 66 years old and let's do a little bit of math and figure out how many years it would take us to break even by waiting until Full Retirement Age to collect benefits.

- $1849.50 times 12 equals $22,194. (That's how much you collect a year at age 62.)

- $22,194 times four years equals $88,776. (That's how much income you will give up by waiting four years to reach FRA.)

- The difference between our primary insurance amount and 75% of our primary insurance amount is $616.50 per month. If we divide that into $88,776 we get 144 months.

That means that if you wait until your full retirement age to collect your benefits, it will take twelve years to make up for the four years that you did not collect. If you wait to collect your benefits until full retirement age, as in our example, you won't make up for the four lost years until you are 78 years old. Granted, every month thereafter you will receive an additional $616.50 (plus any cost-of-living adjustments) for the rest of your life. While there are many factors involved in strategies that maximize your Social Security benefits: your health, your genetics, and your feelings about how long you think you're going to live should be a part of the formula. We also consider factors like taxes, whether you are still employed, and your spouse's Social Security status when we try to determine the best age for taking Social Security income.

Lately, I've seen many articles in the press virtually shouting at people with headlines such as: "Don't commit the mistake of collecting Social Security at 62 years old!" Let's keep in mind that every month you delay claiming benefits is a month without a check. Certainly there is no blanket right or wrong when it comes to making the very personal choice of when to begin collecting your Social Security monthly benefits. While I will go on in this chapter to talk about the advantages of delaying the collection of your benefits I want you to know that I am not advocating that deferring your benefits is necessarily the right decision for you.

It is also important to note that you can defer taking Social Security benefits until you are 70 years old. As baby boomers work longer into their 60s this becomes an important factor in deciding whether to delay benefits. Every year that you wait to collect benefits after your full retirement age will result in a higher monthly check, and just as collecting at age 62 results in a lower number for the rest of your life, deferring until age 70 results in a higher number for the rest of your life. Each year after full retirement age will earn you delayed credits that work out to be about 8% per year until age 70. It's important to note that you cannot earn delayed credits after age 70, so there really isn't much reason to defer payments any longer. Why would someone delay? There may be tax implications by taking the benefits while still working, or the person may want to make sure that his spouse gets the maximum survivor or spousal benefit. We'll talk more about that in a minute.

Widows and Divorcees

Any discussion of collecting SS benefits will include questions about what happens to divorced and widowed claimants. And I'm happy to tell you, for the most part, the Social Security system is very inclusive.

Let's talk about divorce first. (In the interest of shorthand I'm going to talk about "she" when it comes to a surviving or divorced spouse although I am fully aware that surviving or divorced spouses come in both genders; it's just cumbersome to keep writing he/she.) If you were married to somebody for 10 years you qualify to collect spousal benefits. And if you were married to three different people for 10 years each, you will have the ability to select the highest available spousal benefit. I'm going to talk more about spousal benefits in a minute because it's an important part of any Social Security maximization strategy. For now, let's say that, if you have the documentation to prove you were married to someone for 10 years, you may claim spousal benefits without their consent, or even knowledge. Your ex-husband doesn't have any control over your Social Security choices, doesn't need to sign off on them, and doesn't lose any of his own benefits based upon your choices. (Doesn't that avoid a series of awkward conversations?)

Surviving spouses have a slightly different, but no less accommodative, set of rules. If your spouse dies you can apply for survivor benefits as early as age 60 (even earlier if you are disabled, and I could write another book on Social Security disability). Keep in mind that the formulas used to determine your monthly benefits are based on your spouse's age, whether they were collecting benefits or not, and your age. For example, if your husband died after he had begun to collect benefits at age 62, your benefit will be based upon the formula used to calculate his benefit. If he had waited until age 70 to begin collecting benefits then your benefit will be based on that larger number. Next the formula uses your age and life expectancy to determine your monthly benefit. Just like in our example above you will get less per month if you claim at a younger age.

I'll give you an example of why delaying collecting your Social Security benefits until age 70 is a tremendous benefit to your spouse. Let's say that a husband, age 68, has not begun to collect Social Security yet and doesn't plan to until age 70 because his wife, who is 10 years younger, is still working. They have other investments and enough income, so Social Security is not needed. When he finds out that he has a serious illness, it might seem logical for him to begin collecting Social Security payments immediately, so he can get what he can out of the system while he is alive. Actually, it will benefit his wife more if he defers: her spousal benefit will be based upon his age when he dies. So if our hero dies at age 70 his wife will be entitled to survivor benefits that are based upon his Full Retirement Age plus the annual 8% delayed credits per year, or 132% of his full retirement benefit. For the rest of her lifetime the widowed spouse will receive a monthly benefit based upon this larger number. (It should be noted that these benefits will max out for her at Full Retirement Age and there are no delayed credits on survivor benefits; so there would be no benefit for her to wait to collect spousal benefits until age 70, she should collect when she reaches Full Retirement Age to maximize her benefits.)

Maximization Strategies

So did I lose you yet? Financial books are hard enough to read, but getting into an in-depth discussion of Social Security benefits is not exactly a gripping read. For the most part, my eyes glaze over when I try to read government regulations, complicated tax codes, or the instructions to assemble IKEA furniture. However, when it comes to finance, I like a lot of moving parts, and one of the most fascinating things about financial planning is that there are so many variables. I really enjoy doing a financial plan when a couple comes in with his and her children, property spread out across many states, complicated tax scenarios, and all of the other intricacies of modern life. Social Security gives us the opportunity to make certain choices that will help us get the most out of your Social Security benefits; let's talk about them.

Depending upon how much other income you earn, your Social Security benefits might be taxed. The tax is based not only on earned income from your job but income from pensions, investments, and even tax-free municipal bonds. Let's stop right there; the government has figured out a way to tax us on tax-advantaged municipal bonds. Go back and re-read that please. Tax free municipal bonds are now taxed via the formula that is used to compute the tax on Social Security.

(I'm not a conservative Tea Party guy, and I'm pretty sure that no one has told them about this form of taxation, but wouldn't it be fun if we did?) You take all of the income I just mentioned (including the tax free interest on tax-free municipal bonds) and then add one half of your Social Security benefits. This is called your combined income, and if it exceeds $32,000 (married filing jointly) or $25,000 (single), up to 50% of your benefits will be taxed as income! If your combined income exceeds $44,000 if married filing jointly or $34,000 if single; up to 85% of your benefits will be taxed! If you are married filing separately, 85% of your benefits will be taxable no matter how much other income you have. It should be noted that these threshold amounts were set in 1983 and have not been adjusted for inflation. As Social Security has increased over the years, and as inflation has eaten into its purchasing power, our SS Benefits are taxed at relatively low income levels. The only way to minimize this tax is to either reduce other income (and there are some financial planning strategies that do this) or to defer collecting Social Security. It's estimated that one third of current Social Security recipients pay income taxes on their benefits. This is a rather unique tax event since one could argue that we already paid taxes to fund our Social Security benefits; we are being taxed on our taxes.

While we're on the subject of reasons to defer collecting Social Security benefits, we should talk about what happens if you collect Social Security and continue to work before retirement. Since so many baby boomers are not retiring before age 66 you may run into this one: if you are collecting Social Security benefits and are younger than Full Retirement Age, your benefits can be reduced. In 2013 the earning test was $15,000 per year or $1260 a month: for every two dollars you earn over the earnings test amount, one dollar in benefits will be withheld. Put that in perspective. You are retired and bored you; are only 63 years old. So you get a job piloting the steamboat at your local theme park. If you earn more than $15,000 a year in this job you will lose a proportional amount of your Social Security benefit. I can hear you now, I paid for my Social Security benefits throughout my career, and now I have to give it back? What's up with that?

In truth, you don't really lose those benefits. When you reach Full Retirement Age, your benefit is recalculated to leave out the months in which the benefits were withheld. Essentially, this cancels out the actuarial reduction for the months you made over the limit. This will still affect you negatively in the long run, so any retirement planning has to involve plans for collecting Social Security income while you are still employed. Practically speaking, it is impractical to collect Social Security benefits while you are still employed if you are under Full Retirement Age.

Please don't let the annual earnings test discourage you from working. The more money you earn, the more money you will have. Social Security does not "penalize" you for working. Once the adjustment is made, you will end up with a higher benefit for the rest of your life. And, of course, the earnings themselves will contribute to your financial well-being. To avoid the earnings test entirely, just wait until you are full retirement age or later to apply for benefits.

Once you hit full retirement age you can earn any amount from working, and no benefits will be withheld. Of course; you will still have that Social Security tax to deal with. This is a good place to tell you that if you receive a pension benefit from a former employer, your Social Security benefits are not affected as long as you contributed to Social Security. Distributions from 401(k)s, and IRAs, also do not affect Social Security benefits, although they do, of course, affect Social Security taxation.

Verify Your Earnings:

Go to the website www.SocialSecurity.gov/mystatement and enter your personal information, and you will find a Social Security benefit statement. While mistakes are very rare, they have been known to happen (especially if you are self-employed) so you'll want to check the accuracy of your historical earnings. Before you retire, I recommend that you see if there is any way to enhance your earnings history. Since the Social Security primary insurance amount is based upon your 35 best years of earnings it is a good idea to look and see if you have any years that are zero or very low income among your top 35 years. If you had gaps or low earning years it might be better for you to wait a few years to retire and continue working so you can get some of the zeros out of your calculation. When my clients come into my office (or have set up a phone appointment) I will ask that they either bring along or transmit a copy of their Social Security benefit statement; it's one of the most important factors in retirement planning.

Income Tax Planning

So if the first key to Social Security maximization is making sure that your benefit statement is accurate, the second key is to make sure you're not getting taxed on your Social Security benefits. This may involve delaying receiving benefits, or it may mean putting certain assets in asset classes that do not trigger the Social Security taxation. For example, if we know that municipal bonds are paying a relatively low interest rate and are still going to be figured into the computation of income taxes, we might decide to find a more appropriate type of investment for those assets.

Coordinate Spousal Benefits

Our goal, when working with a married couple, is to use both of the couples' Social Security benefits to maximize their strategies. This will make a difference not only during their lifetimes; but also to the surviving spouse after one of them dies. It requires asking the right questions and, in my case, using my really nifty Social Security calculator to come up with a strategy that is the most efficient. One of the most useful strategies is something we call "File and Suspend," it's designed to maximize the higher earning spouse's income while providing immediate income to the lower earning spouse. I borrowed this strategy from the Center for Retirement Research at Boston College; the good Jesuits have always been known to have subversive qualities when it comes to taxation. It works like this: a lower earning spouse can only collect spousal benefits when the higher earning spouse has applied for benefits himself. So let's say that we have a couple who are the same age, 66 years old. The husband will file for his benefits and then ask that the benefit be suspended. This will allow his spouse to begin to collect her full spousal benefit. Note: the spouse who is filing and suspending his benefits must be at full retirement age (FRA) for the strategy to work. The older spouse then waits until age 70 to collect his own benefit, at which time he has maxed out the available monthly check. The spousal benefit is 50% of the higher earning spouse's benefit, and it is part of the planning process for us to determine which spouse is the higher earning claimant. Again, the spousal benefit is based upon the claimant's age and the spouse's age. The benefit of the strategy is not only the immediate cash flow to the household, but if the higher earning spouse should predecease the other she will be able to claim his higher benefit for the rest of her life.

Claim Now, Claim More Later

This opportunity to utilize this strategy is a little rarer, but still potentially very powerful. In this strategy the higher earning spouse claims his spousal benefit when he reaches full retirement age. Of course; his spouse must have already filed and be receiving benefits. Now the higher earning spouse will receive a monthly check from the time he reaches full retirement age until he turns age 70 at which time he will switch to his own higher and maxed out benefit. Both the Claim Now Claim More Later strategy and the File and Suspend strategy have become increasingly popular as baby boomers work until their 70s and as we find that men and women are both bringing substantial earnings records to their retirement.

There are many other strategies for maximizing Social Security, and that's why I insist on doing comprehensive financial planning for my retired clients, not just looking at their investments, or just their insurance, or just their estate plan. I'll talk more in a future chapter about what happens when you turn 70 ½ and how you have to take required minimum distributions from your retirement accounts. Through comprehensive planning you can begin to see how these distributions will affect your taxes and your tax on your Social Security earnings. Sometimes, planning years ahead can minimize taxes. You should begin to see your retirement in a comprehensive and holistic view. Social Security, healthcare, the expenses of living in a home, travel, new vehicles, and about 1 million other moving parts are the variables that make everyone's retirement plan unique and personal.

Today we deal with retirees who have been married several times and who have separate sets of children to consider when it comes to estate planning and even a choice of spouses when it comes to selecting which Social Security benefits from which they draw. Social Security is a powerful and constant source of income throughout retirement, and the decisions that you make as you begin drawing money from the system will have an effect on the rest of your life and perhaps your spouse's.

The Social Security trust fund is continuing to grow as the second half of Baby Boomers approach 65 and continue to add their withholdings to the fund. Since Social Security is a pay-as-you-go system, the fund will be able to meet its obligations until the year 2033, about 18 years from now. At that point it is projected that Social Security will only be able to pay 77% of its current benefits. Like most Americans; I do not have a lot of faith in our politicians or their ability to handle any upcoming crisis. When it comes time to decide whether I want to start collecting benefits at age 62 or wait until age 70 I would be mistaken if I did not say that my faith in our future politicians' ability to make tough decisions is part of my decision-making process. The resolution of the future Social Security crisis will require either an increase in Social Security taxation, raising the full retirement age (FRA), or reduced cost of living adjustments. It is no wonder that Social Security benefits are commonly called the third rail of American politics, Baby Boomers will still be a powerful voting block when it is finally the Social Security System's day of reckoning.

Did you ever see a clown in the circus juggle while standing on top of a big beach ball? That's kind of the way I think of retirement planning. In making plans for your own retirement you must consider your available current benefits, what happens if you delay them, and if you feel confident that the benefits will be there for you in the future. You have to do this while planning around your current income tax circumstances, your projected income tax circumstances, your income needs, your projected income needs, your and your spouse's expected life expectancy, and a host of other factors no computer software can pinpoint for you. The important thing is that you can't really go backwards once you've made a Social Security decision. You can't start taking your distributions at age 62 and then expect at age 70 to get the distribution you would've gotten had you deferred your payments. It doesn't work that way! Once you decide to start taking your payments, your future payments, and perhaps your spouse's will be set at a certain level and will only be increased by cost-of-living adjustments. It is important to note that those cost-of-living increases are a percentage applied to your monthly benefit, and the person with a higher monthly benefit will end up with more dollars in an annual increase than a person with a lower benefit. There are many good arguments for delaying Social Security until you can max out the benefit, and there probably are just as many good arguments for taking the benefit just as soon as you can. A good retirement plan should consider all of your social security planning options.

As we begin to examine the sources of income in retirement we consider Social Security a "permanent" form of income. We don't have the option to take a lump sum instead of a monthly income, and we know that the payments will come to us for the rest of our lives. So like a traditional pension plan, we build a retirement plan around the framework of a maximized Social Security benefit. Let's see what else goes into that calculation.

5

THE BINS AND GAPS APPROACH TO RETIREMENT PLANNING

**Lady Willpower, it's now or never
Give your love to me...
Gary Puckett and the Union Gap**

The biggest fear of anyone seriously considering retirement is that you might run out of money. Even the most well pre-pared retirees live with the fear that they may outlive their assets and be left to the mercies of others as they enter their later years of life. I've developed some calculations that will help you to understand if you have enough retirement assets to retire, right now, and a method for investing those funds that allows you to keep your current cash flow appropriately invested while investing the assets you'll need later in retire-ment in asset classes that have traditionally done better over more meaningful periods of time.

Since we already examined your retirement cash flow needs (your ARB or Anticipated Retirement Budget), we will now begin to examine the sources of income that may potentially support your lifestyle. In my method of retirement planning, we'll take the most conservative possible view of retirement income and begin by looking only at your guaranteed lifetime income, like your Social Security check and any other pension type payments that you may be lucky enough to have. I don't count anything else as a permanent source of income—not rental property (it might be sold or condemned), not interest payments on bonds (they eventually mature), not the funds in your retirement accounts. We'll account for these assets in the next step, but the question I want to have answered at this point is whether this guaranteed income covers the expenses of your ARB. If you can live on Social Security income and other guaranteed income, then you have other areas on which to focus than someone who has an income "gap" and needs to depend upon his other financial assets to maintain his retirement lifestyle.

As I write this book in early 2015, the conditions under which baby boomers are expected to make lifetime decisions about their retirements could not be more hazardous if designed in a laboratory. As the first generation to retire with sizable 401(k) or other types of retirement plan balances, we risk loss of principal if we make the wrong call on investing in stocks, bonds, or any other type of financial asset. A bad market could takes years to recover from, and the alternative—locking our funds in a lifetime monthly income through an insurance company annuity—seems like a bad idea in light of current low interest rates. Why lock in a lifetime income based on historically low interest rates? These conditions would stump an actuary or a professional money manager, much less the individual investor who has been given the responsibility of managing his or her money for the rest of his or her life.

I developed the Bins and Gaps approach to financial planning as a direct response to the problems the retiree faces today. It emphasizes flexibility, long-term planning, and the safety of immediate cash flow. It's been my experience that it is easier to keep a long-term perspective on investments if your immediate cash flow needs are not subject to the volatility of the financial markets. While Wall Street seems to be rather proud of coming up with complicated and arcane strategies to manage your money, I tend to be of the school that says, "If I can't explain an investment strategy to you on a bumper sticker then you shouldn't buy it." I think once you grasp the concept of the Bins and Gaps approach, you will have one of those "I could've had a V-8" moments and wonder why you didn't think of this yourself. The truth is, I wonder why I didn't think of a lot sooner! And the reason I didn't think of this sooner was that for most of our adult lives interest rates were significantly higher and it was easy to take them for granted! Are we going to return to higher rates, or are the current conditions the new normal? It doesn't really matter; a good retirement plan should have the flexibility to cover all contingencies.

For a long time it was safe to live on the interest income from your investments without invading principal, but in today's market environment, with low interest rates and a relatively high stock market, it is almost impossible to plan your retirement on interest income alone. The idea of "never touching principal" isn't so foreign to retirees anymore because interest rates are so low that it's almost impossible to conceive of living a comfortable retirement while earning almost no interest on your saved funds. The current economic environment has forced all of us to become investors instead of savers and that should be more than a little frightening to someone getting ready to retire. Let's talk a little bit about that concept of saving versus investing.

"Investing" involves some degree of risk-taking by the investor while "savings", pretty much does not. A few decades ago, when I defined "savings," I was saying that I pretty much have all the money I want or need, and I simply want to place it somewhere where I can earn a better return than the current inflation rate with no risk to principal. (You might remember your Grandparents getting 10% interest in insured certificates of deposit!) The trouble is, here in the new normal, the inflation rate is close to zero, and the corresponding interest rates for risk-free investments is close to zero also. An investor, on the other hand, is someone who is trying to build wealth and earn a commensurate return on his funds to the risk he has assumed. Currently the lack of reward for savers has necessitated that they become accidental investors. These individual investors, during retirement, are encouraged to take risks with their money that may force them to experience consequences that they were not ready to endure. The stock market is not a money machine, despite the Wall Street propaganda, all stock market investing involves risk.

When you consider that many baby boomers are being forced into the stock market because they have not done an adequate job of setting aside funds for their retirement, you have the perfect storm in place to cause the next Great Depression. If the financial assets that make up the bulk of most 401(k) plans and IRA rollovers were to be exposed to a monumental fall in value, an entire generation will be left impoverished. On the other hand, what is the alternative? Baby boomers feel that if they don't take some degree of risk they will not be able to live the retirement lifestyle that they feel entitled to. These are rocky waters that require expert navigation.

If you know a little bit about the history of economics, then you know that everything is cyclical. Today's high interest rate environment might turn into tomorrow's record low interest rates. The stock market that looks like it is roaring to new heights can turn on a dime and leave investors frightened and even a little broke. Trying to tell the future, no matter how educated your guess, is useless if you guess wrong. I'm going to suggest that there's a better way to invest than depending upon past performance, computer simulations, and educated guesses.

The Bins and Gaps approach to retirement planning helps you to maintain the flexibility to adjust to any economic environment you may encounter during your entire retirement. When used in conjunction with comprehensive financial planning, the Bins and Gaps approach is designed to adjust to inflation and replenish principal that you may need to spend to keep up your lifestyle. As I mentioned, it's almost impossible to plan for retirement without considering spending some principal, and the goal of this approach to retirement planning is to replace the principal with future growth. As you'll see, the Bins and Gaps approach to retirement planning is an easy to visualize and simple to adjust method of deploying your retirement assets.

You and Managing Risk

If you read a financial planning textbook, you will see that risk is defined by the volatility of a particular asset or asset class. If I have a stock that has fluctuated regularly in price between $20 and $80, it is considered more risky than one that sits steadily between $40 and $50. Historically, the more volatile asset classes might prove to perform better over time; but the retiree who is dependent upon volatile assets for his income will probably endure more stress than he'd prefer. The Bins and Gaps approach uses fixed or low risk investments for the current years of retirement while setting aside dollars for the more volatile (and potentially higher returning) assets for later years.

To repeat, the three hallmarks of the Bins and Gaps approach are flexibility, long-term planning, and safety of immediate cash flow. You'll see that we accomplish this by dividing your retirement assets into 5 Year Bins, with the money you need in the first years of retirement being invested ultra-conservatively and subsequent bins being invested in more volatile assets that traditionally do better over longer periods of time. Flexibility allows retirees to respond to changes in their lifestyle or the economic environment. For example, if interest rates should return to more "normal" levels retirees should have the flexibility to move a portion of their assets into fixed and lower risk investments that may be paying a higher rate of return. Of course, higher interest rates usually come with their own set of consequences, and investors may have to make other adjustments to their portfolios to compensate. Clients who lose a spouse or go through health challenges may have to adjust their standard of living upwards or downwards to respond to changes in their life. By retaining flexibility in their portfolio design, they will have the ability to make these changes. Right now, for example, retirees have the ability to purchase a guaranteed lifetime income from an insurance company that is known as a "fixed immediate annuity." The factors that determine this lifetime income are life expectancy, based on age, and current interest rates which makes these annuities not quite as attractive as they once were. But retirees who wait to purchase this type of income might find that they can get more income for their investment dollar if interest rates are higher and when they are older. The Bins and Gaps retirement plan design retains the flexibility to make changes.

Right now, retirees who are not doing comprehensive retirement planning—such as the Bins and Gaps method—are forced to choose between short-term safety and long-term growth, or, at very least, hope that they've made very good assumptions about the economy going forward. The long-term planning component of the Bins and Gaps retirement plan design divides your retirement portfolio into five-year increments that we call "Bins." The first Bin, which is invested only in insured or otherwise low risk investments, is designed to provide a dependable monthly income. During the time that you are spending down this Bin, the rest of your portfolio is working to give you more income in the future and, hopefully, replace the principal which you have spent during the first five years. By removing the first five years of income from investment risk you are automatically building in a discipline that allows you to take a longer-term approach with the rest of your assets. Individual investors have historically been poor market timers and having a longer-term approach to investing usually pays off.

The liquidity of immediate cash flow design feature of the Gaps and Bin retirement approach means that your current cash flow only comes from low risk investments. Often we suggest that you take the first five years of anticipated cash flow and invest those dollars in a series of short term certificates of deposit or short term investment-grade bonds that come due each year (a laddered portfolio). The interest earned on each of these instruments will serve as a small increase in income and provide cost-of-living adjustments to your income. The subsequent bins are invested in asset classes that are historically better performers over meaningful periods of time. It is beyond the scope of this book to recommend specific investments or asset classes to you. (Please note that bonds are subject to interest rate risk and interest rate risk if sold prior to maturity. Bond values will decline as interest rates rise and bonds are subject to availability and change in price. Bond yields are subject to change. Certain call or redemption features may exist which could impact yield.)

Retirees utilizing the Bins and Gaps retirement approach have the option of rolling a percentage of their assets forward every year so that they always have five years of cash on hand, or they may choose to wait until well into the fourth year to make their next adjustments. There is nothing magical about five-year Bins: four-year Bins, or six-year Bins will probably work fine. The important thing is to have the discipline to stick with this approach. I also strongly recommend that my clients monitor their spending habits and plans on a regular basis, and at least annually we should take an objective and unemotional examination of the dollars invested and how long they will last at the current rate.

In order to teach this concept to you, I've used quite a few terms that you might find in a lot of investment literature. It will be useful to review them here:

Projected Retirement Budget: before you retire it is crucial that you have an idea of what your monthly expenses are and have some sort of plan as to how you will spend money going forward. The person who takes a distribution from a 401(k) and then decides to make all kinds of large purchases may find that he doesn't have enough assets to last through retirement. Preparing a budget and having the willpower to stick to it is the only way that I know of to make retirement planning work. If you aren't going to have a retirement budget you probably don't need to read the rest of this book.

Gaps: this term refers to the difference between your guaranteed monthly income from sources like Social Security and any pensions that you might have in your retirement budget. Your gap could reflect a monthly surplus or a monthly deficit. We are, of course, more concerned with a deficit, our charge is to fill our monthly gap over time and invest our funds in a manner consistent with replacing the funds we've spent to maintain our lifestyle.

Lifetime Gap: the lifetime gap is a measure, in today's dollars, of how big (or small) your monthly gap is when we extended over your life expectancy. Although our national life expectancy is somewhere around 80 years old, I prefer to use an age expectancy of 100 when preparing a financial plan, but you may choose to pick a younger or later age when preparing your own plan. So for example, if I have a $200 difference between my projected retirement budget and my Social Security income, and I am 65 years old, then I would calculate my lifetime gap by multiplying $200×12 (months)× 35 (years) to reach a figure of $84,000 as a lifetime gap. If I currently have $84,000 or more in my retirement accounts then I have a "funded" retirement. If I don't, my retirement is "Unfunded."

Funded vs. Unfunded Retirement: This simple calculation projects your monthly Gap over your life expectancy and asks a simple question: do you have enough money in your retirement plan accounts, right now, to pay off your Lifetime Gap? If you do, congratulations, you have a "Funded Retirement." If you don't, be careful; you have an "Unfunded Retirement." It should be noted that a Funded Retirement is not that same as a "paid up" retirement; an unexpected event, such as a major purchase or a bad investment experience, can easily create an Unfunded Retirement where you once had a Funded Retirement. Even a Funded Retirement requires vigilance; you need to keep up with inflation and taxes throughout your life.

Bins: Bins are an accounting device used to segment your retirement plan assets into groups of five years. Your first Bin includes the assets needed to fill your annual gap for the first five years of retirement, your second Bin years 6-10... etc. While you don't have to actually divide your funds into separate accounts for each Bin, I would be sure to create a spreadsheet to identify each of your investments and which Bin they are designed for. Typically, we invest in increasingly less conservative investments per Bin.

Life Expectancy: we base our calculations on your estimated life expectancy. While living to 100 years old might seem overly optimistic, I'd rather ere on the side of caution. If we use a life expectancy of 80 years, as is the national average, your assets might do a better job of filling your gap, but on the other hand, living without any money left over is a bad plan.

Principal: I like to think of principal as the current value of your retirement accounts and the value of it at the beginning of every year after that. While we consider a fully Funded Retirement one that has enough principal to last you until age 100; it is hoped that our investment results will replenish spent principal as you empty each Bin and begin to use the next one. It's not unrealistic to imagine that you may live well beyond your hundredth birthday, and if we have been able to replenish principal during your retirement you will have assets remaining to pass on to whomever you'd like.

Retirement Accounts: for the purpose of this book and the Gaps and Bin approach to retirement planning, I think of retirement accounts as a tax-deferred account like a 401(k), 403B, IRA, IRA rollover, or Roth IRA. It may also include life insurance, annuities, and any other account that allows systematic and regular withdrawals. For that reason, I don't usually think of real estate, even dependable income producing commercial real estate, as retirement accounts for no particular reason other than they're not really liquid. If you decide that one of the Bins in your retirement plan should include commercial real estate, I have nothing against that, but in this book I'm primarily talking about tax qualified retirement plans. And if you have a lot of assets that are set aside from your retirement plan, I am happy for you; I don't usually include such non-retirement assets in your retirement plan calculations when it comes to determining your

Gap. (You can, if you need to, but since retirement accounts usually have to be liquidated over your life expectancy, I use them first when filling Gaps.) It's been my experience that people who are independently wealthy and have assets outside of the retirement plans can still benefit from the Bins and Gaps approach to retirement planning. Budgeting, orderly liquidation of assets, and tax planning suggest that utilizing retirement plan assets for retirement is an efficient method of managing retirement; and using non-retirement assets for estate planning, charitable donations and major purchases is often more efficient.

Base Income: I think of base income as income that will be paid to you for life, guaranteed, and with no options other than to accept an income. Social Security income, government pensions, or other annuitized payments are examples of the base income. In a married couple, if one spouse continues working part-time while the other is completely retired, we will take that income into consideration when calculating the Lifetime Gap and understand that our annual reviews might have to be adjusted if that employment comes to an end. I don't usually include investment income from stock dividends, or bond interest, or even rental real estate income into my base income projection because any of these assets could be sold, or the income might stop due to circumstances beyond our control. I would rather use these forms of income as a means to fill in the monthly gap.

Fully Funded Retirement: if the assets in your retirement accounts are greater than your projected lifetime gap we can say that you have a fully Funded Retirement. That means that if your projected budget is accurate, and you earn a rate of return equal to increases in the cost of living, then you have enough assets on hand to retire. Of course, if you spend more than your budget, or if you lose money in your investments, your Funded Retirement can become Unfunded at any time.

Fully funded does not mean that your retirement is guaranteed; it simply means that you have enough assets on hand to meet future anticipated expenses.

Unfunded Retirement: if the assets in your retirement accounts are less than your projected lifetime gap we say that you have an Unfunded Retirement. What we mean by that is that you don't have enough assets on hand to meet anticipated expenses. Unless you lower your expenses or increase your assets, you will run out of money. Sometimes, when we find that retirement has too large a gap, we suggest that you defer retirement. Deferring retirement gives you the opportunity to save assets and perhaps collect a larger monthly Social Security check. Retiring with a large unfunded balance puts pressure on you to reach for riskier investment returns or potentially run out of assets while you are still alive. The LAST thing any responsible Retirement Planner would suggest is that you lower your life expectancy to make the formula work. Planning to run out of assets once you are significantly into retirement is, in actuality, the opposite of "planning."

Annual Review: let's say you're about 60 years old, and the last time you took a look at your personal budget was when you were 21 years old. It might be rather difficult to figure out how a $30,000 car would fit into your 1979 budget. Well, with a little bit of luck, diet, and exercise (and the ability to avoid getting on the wrong side of Liam Neeson), it's not inconceivable that you can live another 40 years or more. It's a pretty safe bet that there will be changes in your cost-of-living along the way, and the only way to make sure that the Bins and Gaps method of retirement planning works is if you review it annually. Fundamental changes in the economy, and changes in interest rates might make recommended changes obvious if you set aside time to review your assets and your budget. As we've mentioned, expenses for things like vacations and major purchases tend to go down as you grow older, but expenses for things like healthcare tend to go up.

Discipline: we sometimes think of the word discipline as meaning "punishment" when, actually, the history of the word goes back to the word "disciple," which means "follower." When it comes to money, having discipline is a virtue. It's entirely possible to mess up a good thing; I can testify to that. And just because you initially have a fully Funded Retirement that does not mean you can go crazy and go off budget. Lack of discipline and not having the ability to say "no" to people who want to borrow your money, or trying to live up to somebody else's lifestyle, or just being unable to say "no" to yourself, are all ways that a Funded Retirement can suddenly become Unfunded. If you worked hard all of your life, paid your bills, and managed to get by on just a paycheck without the aid of lottery winnings, a trust fund, or holding down two jobs, you should find that adhering to a budget during retirement is no hardship.

So there you have it: you've been introduced to the Bins and Gaps method of retirement planning, a method that is designed to help you stay flexible, keep a long-term view of retirement, and to have the comfort of knowing that your immediate cash flow is in a safe and dependable place. I'm going to go into more detail as we get deeper into the book and I want to talk about the concept of Comprehensive Retirement Planning. Someone, whether it is you, your accountant, your CERTIFIED FINANCIAL Planner™ Practitioner, your attorney, or even your significant other, needs to be the conductor of the financial orchestra that is your life. Retirement planning is about more than Bins and Gaps: a good financial plan should take into account income taxes, major and unexpected costs, healthcare, income tax planning, and estate planning. Nothing should be done in a vacuum; someone, preferably professional, should be looking at the big picture when it comes to your finances. In short, you need "a guy." I don't mean a man versus a woman, I mean a guy as in "I'll ask my guy." Who is your go-to guy? I'd like to think that my clients think I am that guy, not just the guy who handles their investments, or does their financial plan, but they also think of me as a trusted family advisor. I'd like to suggest that if you don't have a trusted family advisor that you find one; you can ask your friends, check the website for the CFP board, or look for some other professional that specializes in elder law and retirement planning.

Now, let's talk a little more about those Gaps.

6

MIND THE GAP

**I don't know, I've got gaps, she's got gaps,
together we fill gaps.
Rocky**

In England, train conductors warn passengers to be careful of the space between the platform and the train car by shouting. "Mind the gaps!" In planning your retirement the concept of Mind Your Gap has a different meaning altogether; we're talking about the disparity between your Anticipated Retirement Budget and your base income. In this chapter we are going to talk about a few ideas to use your assets to increase retirement income with an eye towards preserving as much principal as possible.

If you recall, in the last chapter, I gave you a back of the envelope formula to determine your gap between anticipated income and anticipated expenses in retirement. The formula looks like this:

Anticipated Retirement Budget–Social Security income and pension income = your Gap.

I also asked you to multiply that gap times 12 months, to annualize it, and then multiply it by the number of years it takes you to reach 100 years old. This formula is sort of like a gas gauge, it quickly tells you if you have enough money to last until you reach 100 years old. While this is a pretty useful number, good financial planning requires many more calculations and decisions. If you do have enough money to fill your gap for the rest of your life, and if inflation is never an issue in your particular world, then you could simply spend your money as you withdraw systematically over the course of your lifetime. Yes, you'd be spending your principal, and if you live to be older than 100 years old you'll be out of money, but at least you know that you will have a somewhat comfortable retirement. Let me say right here, running out of money, at any time during your life, is not a good thing, and we strive to avoid this fate. But in making your initial retirement planning decisions, we have to start somewhere! The important thing is this: if you have enough financial assets on hand to fill your gap for the rest of your life, your approach to money management becomes one of conservation of principal and keeping up with inflation while striving to replace the assets you are using to support your lifestyle. In my mind, that's a different approach than if you have a large gap that requires you to reach for higher annual returns to support your standard of living.

In real life, retirement planning consists of many more variables than our simple back of the envelope calculation. For one thing, your expenses might go up or they might go down. Hopefully you'll continue to evolve as a person during retirement, and you may take up new pursuits that require you to spend more money or perhaps less. (In my life, for example, I've replaced the relatively expensive hobby of boating with the relatively inexpensive hobby of road cycling. Now instead of tanks of gas and docking fees, I buy electrolyte supplements for my water and padded lycra shorts.) A good retirement plan should have the flexibility to allow your income to change as your lifestyle does.

The concept of a Lifetime Gap is a relatively brilliant method of checking in on your assets and spending habits. I like to think of it like this: if I wanted to buy a new road bike, and I had the money to pay cash for said bike in my checking account, my bike is "funded." If I spend the money on something else, or decide to buy a more expensive bike, the proposed purchase is no longer fully funded. In the same way, having an idea as to whether you are embarking upon a Funded or Unfunded Retirement is a mighty useful piece of information! With all the variables of retirement, from life expectancies to changes in your budget, having a simple gas gauge to check on is a convenient and useful tool.

Let's try an example: Joyce is a 65-year-old retiring teacher with $400,000 in her retirement account. Her monthly expenses are relatively low, and all but $500 of her monthly expenses are covered by her teacher's pension and Social Security. When we multiply her $500 a month Gap times 12 months we get an annual Gap of $6000. Our simple little back of the envelope calculation tells us that if she lives to be 100 years old, filling her gap would cost $210,000 by the time she turned 100 years old. Joyce is comfortably set for retirement and can begin to plan to minimize income taxes and make sure that her estate plan is in order. Most importantly, she knows that her Funded Retirement does not require that she take on any more risk than she is absolutely comfortable with as she gets older!

Here's another example: Karen and Michael are a 67-year-old married couple who have saved $500,000 in their 401(k) accounts. Neither has a pension, and their combined Social Security generates almost $3000 a month. Because they still have a mortgage, like to travel, and prefer to drive (and finance) new cars, their Anticipated Retirement Budget of $4000 a month leaves them with a $1000 Gap. That's a $12,000 annual deficit, and using our definition of financial independence, they have a Funded Retirement since they would not spend all of their principal by the time they each reach 100 years old (12,000 X 33 years= $396,000). And their annual deficit is only 2.4% of the value of their retirement accounts, so any annual return over that number would replace the funds they are using to support their lifestyle. Because this is a second marriage for both of them, their planning needs include estate equalization and plans to replace the lost Social Security check if one of them should die. To keep their retirement Funded, they will need to make plans to replace the lost income from Social Security for the survivor while also appeasing the children from each of their marriages who expect an inheritance.

Our final example is a couple who is not quite ready to retire; despite the fact that they would like to: Elaine and Glenn are 62-year-old professionals with about $200,000 in retirement accounts. If they collected Social Security right now they would only collect about $1700 a month. Neither has a pension, and they have five years remaining on their mortgage. Their monthly expenses in retirement are estimated to be about $2500 a month. That's an $800 a month Gap or $9600 a year. If we project them both out to 100 years of age that's $364,800 of excess expenses, well over their $200,000 in retirement accounts. In this case the $9600 in annual excess expense is equivalent to 4.8% of the annual value of the retirement accounts, meaning that if they retired today they would be under pressure to earn almost 5% a year from their accounts to stay above water and not spend principal. I don't think anybody would say this is unreasonable or undoable but compared to our first two examples, Elaine and Glenn would be stretching their portfolio to the limits. Although their financial planner told them that they could retire now, with some risk, he suggested that they wait a few years. In a few years their Social Security checks will be higher, their mortgage will be paid down, and we can even factor in a slightly shorter life expectancy. In addition; they will have an opportunity to put more money in the retirement accounts.

Make no mistake about it, it is not unusual for people to retire without a lifetime of income set aside, and couples like Elaine and Glenn retire all the time with some uncertainty as to whether they will have enough assets to last the rest of their lives. But since we are talking about Retirement Planning, coming up with a good sense of whether we have enough assets to retire safely is more comfortable than the "close your eyes and hope for the best" method of financial planning. Many people today are retiring with unfunded gaps in their monthly budgets, which I believe is fine as long as they have defined how they will fill the Gap. Sometimes that gap requires a change in retirement expectations, downsizing a home, or working part-time in retirement.

The Second Calculation

In the interest of making future plans, I'd like to know how fast I am burning through my assets when I have a Gap; so I apply a second calculation that I alluded to in the examples above. All I want to do is figure out what percentage of my assets I am spending each year. Simply, if I have a $6000 annual Gap, how much of my assets am I burning through each year? If I have $60,000 in an IRA, then I know that I will be spending 10% of the value of my account in the first year. In any year that I make more than 10% on my investments my portfolio grows, in any year that I make less, it goes down. (If I had $600,000 instead, my Gap is only 1% of my portfolio value, a much easier number to work with! Duh.) Like my first calculation, the second calculation is a good barometer of how much return I need to try to attain and how much risk I must assume to get it. Sometimes financial advisors are tempted to tell a client, "oh go ahead and retire; you'll be fine," when in the back of their mind they are saying to themselves,

"I sure hope the market goes up this year." Serious financial plans shouldn't build sand castles that get washed away with the first bear market that comes along; during the course of retirement there will be good and bad markets.

Going back to our Gas Gauge analogy, I control how much gas I use by how hard I push down on the gas pedal. Driving with the throttle wide open is going to burn through gas much more quickly than driving at a reasonable speed. Your retirement portfolio will suffer through bad markets during your retirement, that is unavoidable. You can really only control your rate of withdrawal and try to insulate your portfolio as much as possible by not asking too much of it.

A Rigid State of Flexibility

Flexibility, then, becomes a hallmark of investing for any well planned retirement. I believe it is essential to plan your retirement investments in a manner that allows you to make adjustments for, not only changes in your lifestyle, but changes in the economy. For example, if you took 100% of your retirement savings right now and bought an immediate annuity with a reputable insurance company you would receive an income for life that you cannot outlive. Immediate annuities are sort of like personal pension plans; they provide a worry-free paycheck every month. While annuities may have a place in a good retirement plan; I'm against putting 100% of your money in anything. When you sell all of your principal to an insurance company in exchange for a lifetime income you give up all of your flexibility and the ability to defend the principal or give yourself periodic raises. If you know people who have retired with a traditional pension plan, you know that the idea of living on a "fixed income" is something that is always on their mind. Today's retirement planning should allow for more flexibility than traditional pension plans.

Financial markets, if nothing else, are cyclical. Just as we are experiencing generationally low interest rates at the moment, we remember a time, not long ago, when interest rates were ridiculously high. In our youth, we experienced an economy that saw the ravages of inflation, high interest rates ordered by Fed chief Paul Volcker, and wage and price controls ordered by the government (remember the WIN buttons promoted by President Ford?) And for most of our adult lives we have watched as interest rates fell from these levels. Whether we stay at these historically low interest rates for the rest of our lives is a matter of conjecture, and it seems unreasonable to make retirement plan decisions that do not acknowledge the need for flexibility.

If your Gap is of a manageable size you should be able to take a long-term view to investing. A long-term view is one in which you are able to weather financial storms (and know the difference between storms and tsunamis) while not having your present lifestyle undermined by the financial markets. When I create a retirement plan I build in flexibility by creating a series of "Bins" that break your retirement into four or five year increments. Your first Bin is designed to provide the cash necessary to cover the first several years of your retirement by keeping enough cash or lower-risk, liquid investments on hand to fill your Gap. This allows us to strategically invest the remaining Bins in asset classes that have traditionally done well over longer periods of time, while buffering our immediate cash needs from the short term fluctuations of the financial markets and the economy.

The Bins and Gaps approach is especially helpful while interest rates are so low, and, by placing most of our assets into Bins that will not be touched for 5 years (and longer), we prevent the problems that come along when we lock in too much money at low interest rates. If the cyclical economy presents us with an opportunity to lock in savings in the future, the Bins and Gaps approach allows us to retain the flexibility to do so when interest rates go higher.

Different asset classes tend to perform better in different circumstances, and, tactically, I like the ability to adjust to changing market conditions during retirement. I prefer not to lock in all of my assets in any one asset class, no matter what it is. I always think back to the retired clients and prospective clients I met when I first entered the financial services industry in the 1980s. With the stock and bond markets under pressure, these people were extremely focused on safety of principal and were unwilling to consider any investment other than government guaranteed issues. While this was a sound and reasonable strategy for the times, they suffered as interest rates (and their interest income) fell to record lows in the coming years. A strategy that included some diversification might have benefited them. (Although, of course, there is no guarantee that a diversified portfolio will enhance over-all returns or outperform a non-diversified portfolio. Diversification does not protect against market risk). Their retirement dilemma was the inverse of ours: they sought to avoid the pain of falling stock prices, but in the long run they suffered from not having protection against falling interest rates. They paid for their lack of flexibility with decreasing income. In a following chapter I'm going to talk about the risks of investing when interest rates are going higher, and guess what my strategy is going to be (spoiler alert): diversification and flexibility!

My observation has been that early in retirement you might approach your new life as if you are embarking on a long and wonderful vacation, and as you get older the need to travel (and spend money) seems to decline. Here in central Florida we have a common phrase about retirees returning to the North as they get further into their retirement years. We say, "they went home." I know a lot of retirees who retired to Florida for the sunshine and to live an active lifestyle but who returned to their native cities to be surrounded by family and familiar environments as they get older. I believe a good retirement plan should keep your funds flexible enough to manage any major changes, especially ones like relocation or health issues.

Also, in a later chapter, I'm going to talk about estate planning and, more specifically, the death of your spouse. Quite often when one spouse passes away any pension income he may have had goes away also. Certainly, that spouse's Social Security payments stop. And while the surviving spouse has the opportunity to choose the higher of the couples' Social Security payments, they will lose the lower one. That means that their gap has changed and a good financial plan should plan for this discrepancy.

If you have planned your retirement very conservatively, as I'm suggesting you do, you may have surprisingly good financial returns and find that you are running ahead of schedule. By beginning conservatively, these hoped-for but not guaranteed increases in the value of your retirement account may provide even more flexibility going forward. The strength of basing your retirement on my first back of the envelope calculation is that any return above zero increases your projected retirement portfolio value. And, the reason I love my business, is that, historically, financial assets do increase significantly over meaningful periods of time. If the value of your portfolio increases, you retain the flexibility to increase your standard of living or take care of your surviving spouse and future generations. Of course, if the value of your portfolio decreases, you may need to make some adjustments to your lifestyles.

The Danger of Common Knowledge

When it comes to investing, "common knowledge" is dangerous. Just as everyone knew that the only investment game in town was FDIC insured certificates of deposit in the 1980s, common knowledge today tells us that investing in the stock market is the only way for retirees to stay ahead of inflation. While the stock market has sometimes been a good inflation hedge; periods of extremely high inflation have not been kind to financial assets like stocks. Today we are experiencing extremely low inflation thanks to the outsourcing of jobs to Asia, the elimination of many middlemen by the Internet, and the speed of global communications. Wages and the cost of goods and services have gone down or at least stayed the same around most of the industrialized world. The United States manufacturing base has been decimated by automation and offshore jobs while companies like Walmart and Amazon have replaced local merchants.

Tactically speaking, many investors have been fighting the last war, the war against inflation, by bidding gold up to record highs. Their logic is that there is no inflation now, governments are printing money to keep our financial system afloat after the financial crisis of 2008, and inflation is bound to come roaring back again. Whether we will remain in a low interest rate environment for the rest of our lives, or whether inflation will come roaring back, as some say it is poised to do, remains a question that all investors are trying to answer. It's a relatively safe bet that interest rates will go higher at some point in the future, but when? People have been calling for interest rates to go higher for the last five years, and, instead, they've actually gone lower! In my mind, any time you find yourself trying to predict the future you are on the verge of speculation, and speculation does not belong in a portfolio that is supposed to last the rest of your life. Sure, if we knew the exact date of our death it would remove a lot of uncertainty from the way we manage our money but that's not the way things work. A good portfolio should take a Zen -like view of the world and focus on the reality of *now* while retaining the flexibility to adjust to changing circumstances.

My conservative Bins and Gaps calculation is a useful tool that tells you where you stand in terms of retirement, no matter what return you are earning, since it is based on your current expenses and the current value of your retirement accounts. The method helps to define the risk you will assume while investing and guide you as you make investment decisions for the rest of your life. Hopefully those decisions will be profitable enough to prevent you from spending more of your assets than necessary and provide a cushion if you should live well past your 100th birthday. Professionally speaking, it is prudent to take the most conservative path possible when making retirement decisions. A good retirement plan, as I've said, assumes a 0% return and is pleasantly surprised when your investments do really well. To me, that's a better plan than hoping that you earn an unreasonably high return and having to go back to work!

If you are talking to an investment sales representative, or insurance salesperson, who is basing their calculations on unsustainable or ridiculously high investment returns, be forewarned: your retirement might be at risk. I know many insurance agents who, in the 80s, were projecting 8% or even 10% returns on their annuity sales proposals in perpetuity, and the people who made retirement decisions based on these numbers were disappointed when actual interest rates came down to lower levels. By the same token, if your retirement software, or your online retirement calculator, is telling you that you will have a great standard of living in retirement if you earn an unreasonable market return; you may be sorely disappointed also. The stock market, over meaningful periods of time, has done well, but applying historical statistics to your individual retirement plan might be hazardous.

If you have $100 in the stock market, and the market goes down 30%, the value of your investment is now $70. The next year, if the market goes back up 30%, your remaining $70 has only grown to $91. The simple math and the reality is: in retirement you can't afford to have significant down years without it affecting your standard of living. My segmented, Bin, approach to retirement allows the assets that you do have in stocks to be segregated from the money you are using to support your standard of living and stay invested in the financial markets for meaningful periods of time.

The Times Have Changed

I've been helping people plan retirements for 30 years now; and the latest change in interest rates has caused our industry to re-examine the fundamentals of how we help people to retire. For the initial part of my career, interest rates or market returns were relatively high, and we made assumptions about retirement planning that we can't make any more. We used to take it for granted that someone getting ready to retire could earn enough interest or profit on their investments to fill the retirement gap without spending principal. The years 2001 and 2008 brought us all back to reality and financial professionals (as well as retirees) have to look at retirement a little differently.

For the sake of using round numbers let's say a client had $1 million in retirement assets and felt comfortable withdrawing $80,000 annually because he believed his return would comfortably generate the 8% he needed to maintain his lifestyle. (Let me stress this: this is not a real case, these are not real numbers, and I'm just trying to give you a simple math illustration.) Theoretically; this client could live comfortably for as long as he lived without touching principal, that is, if he earned a minimum of 8% a year. I have to tell you that I remember when 8% in a fixed income product was not very hard to find. Many observers were convinced that the stock market would always return a minimum of 8%, and a lot of software used by professionals and individual investors used similarly high interest rate or stock market return assumptions. When interest rates retreated to today's low levels, retirees, like the man in this example, found that they were forced to invade principal to maintain their lifestyle. It appears, at least for now, that the days of maintaining a high standard of living while living on fixed income investments that are paying a high and safe guaranteed rate are over. Today, it is not unreasonable to expect $1 million in a retirement fund to only generate 1% or 2% interest in fixed income investments that are guaranteed. In today's interest rate environment it might take $10 million to generate $80,000 of annual interest income. So: investors are forced to assume SOME type of risk to maintain their lifestyle, and we are going to talk about risk, in depth, in a later chapter.

So how is anyone supposed to retire using the model that is based on guaranteed investment income? Basically, it's almost impossible for anyone to retire and receive a guaranteed income that maintains their current lifestyle without planning to spend down some principal. And spending principal is not a mortal sin, it's not against nature, and, at least for right now, it's a fact of life. The democratization of retirement planning requires only that we set aside enough assets during our working careers to support ourselves until we die. We are not charged with making sure that those assets are never touched and passed on to future generations. That's putting way too much pressure on ourselves and our retirement lifestyle. I hope that last sentence helped to remove a large load from your shoulders.

If you set enough money aside during your career to fill your Gaps during your life expectancy, you have done everything you've been expected to do. If you earn enough money during retirement to leave some to future generations, or if you've purchased a life insurance policy for that purpose, then you get bonus points. Your major concern, in my opinion, should be to make sure that your funds last for all of your lifetime, and I would be making every decision with the potential longevity of my life in mind. Because of today's relatively low interest rates and relatively risky stock market, the Bins and Gaps approach to retirement should afford you the flexibility to lock in high interest rates if they cycle back around again during your many years of retirement.

Let's talk for a minute about the possibility of really, really high interest rates coming back again. What type of environment leads to very high interest rates? That's an environment that is caused by some sort of financial event that is usually caused by very high inflation. That's not necessarily a positive thing for those of us who are retired. If we have locked ourselves into lifetime incomes (like a traditional pension) that seem to offer reasonable returns in 2015; we might be in for some very hard times in the year 2030. A return to very high interest rates will require as much flexibility in the construction of your portfolio as you need in today's low interest rate environment. Think about it: you won't know if interest rates are about to go higher or lower any better than you do today. You won't know whether to lock in for the long term or wait for even higher rates. By keeping your retirement funds in the 5 year increments that we call Bins, you may have greater flexibility to survive any change in economic circumstances.

So while it is not possible in today's interest rate environment to reasonably live on interest-only from fixed income investments, maintaining flexibility in your retirement account may allow you to return to that strategy if it once again becomes viable. In the meantime, spending as little principal as possible to fill your gap is about the only approach that I think is available to us. At the same time, relying on unrealistic projections for returns in stock-based accounts is also dangerous. I'm not saying that I don't think stocks will go higher; I am suggesting that gambling your life savings on the stock market during retirement is living a lot more dangerously than most of us would like to, and life is not a remake of Casino Royale (and you are not Bond, James Bond.) If you are making high systematic withdrawals from your retirement accounts for living expenses and hoping that the stock market will achieve a high enough return to make up for those withdrawals; you will almost certainly have a year, at some point, that will make your strategy impossible to continue. When you are still working and adding to your retirement accounts you can absorb years of negative returns by potentially having years that make up for them. But when you are withdrawing money for living expenses from your equity accounts, you run the risk of depleting your accounts almost all the way to zero with just a few bad years of investment performance. Going to zero is, by the way, the opposite outcome of successful retirement planning.

The Bin Approach

I've never been to a Christmas tree farm, but I can imagine that the farm is subdivided into plots of trees that are ready for each succeeding Christmas for the next several years. And I would imagine that as one Christmas harvest is sold off it is replanted with seedlings for a harvest in the future. I'm guessing that you're not a farmer and that you've never commercially grown trees either, but if you grasp this concept you will have an insight into The Bin Approach to retirement investing. It works like this: your first five years of retirement is the first crop and is used to fill your retirement gap. Your second five years is the next crop, the third five years the next crop and so on. You design your investments so that the crop that is ready to be harvested is invested in short-term, nonvolatile investments that are not affected by changes in the financial markets. Each succeeding five year Bin is invested in asset classes that have better long-term track records, albeit with more volatility. The five year Bin that I begin with is segregated from my long-term investments and used for cash flow. The succeeding Bins are invested without any pressure of having to fulfill current cash flow needs.

Depending upon the size of your monthly gap and the assets you have to work with, I like to segregate five years of the assets required to fill your monthly gap into the first (or current) Bin which is invested in low risk, short-term investments. We schedule these investments to liquidate monthly, quarterly, or annually to fill your cash flow needs. We may even purchase a five year immediate annuity for this purpose. The important thing is that these funds are not subject to any risk of principal, at all, and are designed to systematically pay themselves down to meet your current cash flow requirements. The segregation of the first five years assets allows us to invest our other Bins into asset classes that traditionally do better over longer periods of time and imme-diately have five years in which we have removed ourselves from the daily turbulence of the financial markets. Instead we have dependable and predictable source of income to fill our gap.

It's time we talked a little bit about money being "fungible." An old client of mine defined fungible by saying "money is money." And what he meant was that if you draw a cup of water from a pail, you still have water in the pail and you still have water in the cup, it's indistinguishable no matter where it's kept. Money works the same way, if I am drawing my living expenses from my entire portfolio every month or from a separate Bin that we have identified as the one we're going to draw from, it doesn't matter. The difference is psychological, mostly, but it goes a little deeper than that. The money that I have segregated into my first Bin is money that I know I am going to spend over the course of the next five years. Since this money is not subject to the fluctuations of the stock market, or the bond market, or the real estate market, or the gold market, etc. I can live with the certainty that my other investments are designed for later on in my retirement. This is more than psychological, it's a forced discipline.

In recent years I have become a road cyclist—you know those guys are always running through red lights on their bicycles with the skinny tires when you have to stop the car like the law-abiding citizen that you are? Yes, I must confess, I wear spandex and I like it! I've been in groups of cyclists that have kept angry motorists from getting to the Krispy Kreme when the "Hot Now" light is on, and I'm proud of it. I have discovered my inner craziness in my later years and revel in it! I ride my bike about 150 miles a week and once a month I ride in a 100 mile ride known as a Century. I love to test my body's endurance, and I especially love that when most reasonable people would say, "I just rode a bike 50 miles; I think I'll go home and rest," I say, "I just rode a bike 50 miles, I'm half way there!" My resulting lifestyle is that I am always in training for the next event, and when I am training I impose a discipline on myself that keeps me from eating the wrong foods or drinking too much alcohol. Calling this lifestyle "training" makes this way of life much easier to stick with than if I called it "diet and exercise." The discipline I impose on myself is strictly my choice and in reality is nothing more than my way of fooling my mind and body into staying in shape. But it works! Imposing a discipline on the way you approach spending your retirement assets is just as important as it is for me to pound up the miles on my bike to maintain my conditioning (and to look good in Lycra).

The simplicity of the Bin approach to retirement planning is that it enforces a discipline on you that might otherwise be difficult to maintain through down markets and periods of personal uncertainty. If you make a commitment to only allow yourself to spend a certain amount of principal during a month, that month turns into a year, which turns into a five-year Bin. At the end of that Bin you start to tap the next Bin and you realize that you have given the assets that you have set aside for the long-term an opportunity to grow. If you were of a mindset that did not separate your assets into five-year Bins, you might find that you are subject to short-term thinking and relative inflexibility. The Bins and Gaps approach to retirement investing allows you to adjust your thinking: you can focus on more meaningful periods of time instead of reacting to daily headlines.

Within the Bins, I still maintain a certain amount of flex-ibility. While I am not trying to be a "market timer," I still think I can recognize major bumps in the road, and I keep the flexibility to get out of the way when things are really bad. And if my needs change, if my gap gets bigger or smaller, I insist on retaining the flexibility to change my strategy. But for the most part, once I put money in a certain Bin, it stays there and, most especially, the first Bin. The first Bin covers the years when I am learning to be retired, so I expect that I will make changes in my spending habits and my lifestyle. It also includes the years in which I am the youngest and most likely to make those changes. But I continue to take the income from those Bins and set any extra income aside to add to my second Bin at the end of the first five years. By withdrawing more than I need during the first five years, I am building a cushion that allows me to handle unexpected expenses without drawing from the funds I'm using for future income, growth of income, or growth.

While it is possible to open separate bank or brokerage accounts for every Bin, more practically the Bins are something I would like to see you keep track of on a spreadsheet, a yellow legal pad, or a note in a safe deposit box. The important thing is that they are written down, labeled, and that somewhere in the margins you have a detailed explanation of what is in each Bin and the timeframe for which it is set aside. For example, if I had shares of a blue-chip stock set aside for Bins three and four, I might keep them in the same brokerage account, but in my notes I will say that a certain percentage of them are designed to be kept in Bin three and the rest for Bin four. In addition to the comprehensive brokerage statement provided by your financial institution, I suggest you also maintain a breakdown of assets by Bins and a timeline of when each Bin is expected to come into use.

Because we have used very conservative estimations to design these Bins, we are perfectly positioned to end up with more in any given Bin than I had expected. And depending on the financial markets, I may find that some Bins are performing below expectations, but because I began with projections of a 0% return, down years, especially if they are in a later Bin, become easier to manage, especially since I am well-diversified. Because the current Bin is always invested in a manner that removes it from market risk, I have no concerns about immediate cash flow.

Depending on the circumstances I may decide during my annual review (and you should always have an annual review) to consider my first Bin to be a rolling Bin and annually take 20% from the next Bin and move it into the cash equivalents in my current Bin. This is kind of an optional, belt and suspenders, approach to retirement cash flow management. If I choose to do this I will likely roll most of my annual surplus (if there is one) into the fifth year of my current Bin. Likewise, if I have an investment that I am particularly fond of (or one that I have high hopes in the future for), I might move it to a Bin that is maturing further in time and substitute the money coming into my current Bin with an asset that I am no longer as enthusiastic about.

The concept of delineating every five years for the rest of your retirement and segregating your investments in a disciplined manner allows your riskier investments to also be your longer-term investments: a concept that allows you to have current cash flow while retaining the flexibility to adjust to changing market conditions. If you look at almost any historical chart of 5- to 10-year rolling returns you will find that historically bad years are overcome by good years. (Past performance is no indication of future results.) And by disciplining yourself not to spend the money that is currently invested in stocks and bonds, you have imposed the discipline on yourself that is metaphorically the same as an athlete in training getting ready for his next event. This approach to retirement planning, when used in conjunction with the computations that tell you your gap and your needed rate of return to fill the Gap are tools that will allow you to take the necessary long-term approach to retirement planning.

How To Restore Your Principal

If you are a little squeamish about running out of money when you hit 100 years old, I feel your pain and I want to share one of the strengths of the Bin approach: you can replenish your Bins! Let's look at a simple math equation: If your gap requires that you spend 3% of your principal to maintain your lifestyle, that means you will run out of money in 33 years if you simply leave your money in mason jars in the back yard. However, I'm assuming that you bought this book because you won't be leaving your money in mason jars and will, instead, put it to work. If you place your first five years of income, or 15% of your assets, in a short term account to supply income, the remaining 85% of your portfolio only needs to earn 3.6% per year for those 5 years to restore the value of your first Bin! Even in today's low interest rate world that's not an unrealistic return and replenishing your Bin increases your options for unexpected expenses, estate planning, or if you decide to live well past your 100th birthday!

We are going to talk a lot more about the Bins and Gaps approach to retirement planning, but I am betting that you are feeling a LOT better about the structure of your retirement plan and how your life will look after you have collected your last paycheck! Me? I'm going out for a bike ride, and when I get back I want to tell you a little bit about a Funded Retirement and then a little more about an Unfunded Retirement. Remember: watch out for cyclists!

7

THE FUNDED RETIREMENT

**I got my hushpuppies on, I guess I never was
made for glitter rock and roll.
Jimmy Buffet**

Stewardship: the careful and responsible management of
something entrusted to one's care.

If you have enough money in your retirement accounts to
cover your Lifetime Gap, we say you have a "Funded Retirement." Of course this number depends upon the accuracy of
your Projected Retirement Budget and your ability to stick
to it. That doesn't mean that you don't have some work to
do or that you can't wind up with no money at some point
in life; it simply means that based on the budget you have
prepared, you currently have enough assets on hand to last
until you turn 100 years old. Your job now is to enact careful
and responsible management of the money that has been
entrusted to your care. In this chapter, I'm going to talk about
some of the things that can go wrong during a Funded Retirement, some of the events you should be ready for, and I'll
reemphasize the vigilance needed in managing your assets
during retirement.

In the good old days of pension plans, a retiree didn't have any decisions to make once he decided to collect his check. Today, it's a lot more complicated, and our retirement plan has many moving parts. Financial planning in general, and retirement planning in particular, is more like Chaos Theory than an exact, measurable science. If we knew for certain the date of your death, the rate of inflation for the rest of your life, the performance of the financial markets, and any major capital expenses that might come along, we could make investment decisions at retirement that would truly mean that you have a fully paid retirement. That's not the way the world works; when we prepare a financial plan we can only make the best decisions that are available to us right now and make annual adjustments that allow for the variables that change along the way. For the most part, a conservatively managed retirement plan that seeks to keep pace with inflation and income taxes can be modified to address your changing needs.

The three areas that you should be most concerned with when managing your retirement funds are: risk management, estate planning, and income taxes. There are also potential major events in your life that could tempt you to raid your retirement funds and decrease the source of your income for the rest of your life. I'm going to talk about each of these and put them in the context of utilizing the investment goals of growth, growth of income, and immediate income. Because I don't have any idea, nor, I'm guessing, do you, as to how the economy or interest rates is going to go over the next 30 or 40 years, I can only suggest that we try to retain flexibility and avoid speculation at all costs. As I mentioned earlier in the book, there is a huge difference between investing and speculating, just as there should be a segregation of your savings dollars and your investment dollars.

The Triad

A comprehensive retirement plan has three goals:

1. Provide Immediate and Sustainable income.

2. Provide Growth of Income

3. Provide Growth of Principal.

THE THREE GOALS OF A COMPREHENSIVE RETIREMENT PLAN

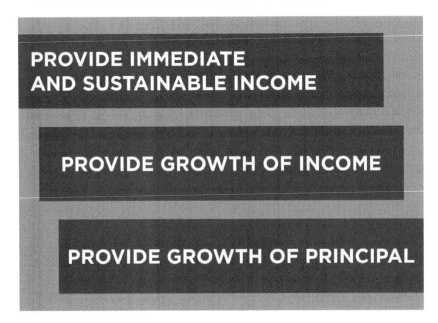

We're going to talk later, in some detail, about the investment design of this portfolio, but let's look at the big picture right now. The most obvious component of the plan is the income part, and not many people would choose to retire if they didn't have enough money coming in to pay the bills; that's understood. The important word is "sustainable' and it is critical, however you generate income, that you have income that you can count on. Let's say, for example, that you had decided to live on the interest from certificates of deposit back when interest rates were high enough to allow for such a thing. Your guaranteed and insured bank deposits might still be worth a lot of money, but their income is almost non-existent today. Planning a sustainable income should involve provisions for almost every economic and personal uncertainty.

The retiree who only lived on the interest from those CD's has experienced the opposite of increased income; a well planned retirement should include periodic increases in income to keep up with the increased cost of living. We expect to be retired for a long time, and no one would start a long term career voluntarily without the hope of a raise. Intuitively, given our current low interest rates, it is logical to hope that a return to more normal interest rates will solve that problem and, if handled properly, that might be true. But investing in a rising interest rate environment is fraught with peril. I've devoted an entire later chapter to this subject; I hope you read it! In addition, people who have been predicting an immediate return to higher rates have been wrong for a while now. Guessing wrong is hazardous when it comes to financial planning.

The final leg of the triad retirement plan is growth. The growth portion of the plan is simply some money set aside for a rainy day. By having some assets segregated from those sending us an income we can be prepared for unexpected major expenses without interrupting our income stream (I often recommend using funds from outside your retirement accounts, if you can, for these expenses, in order to lessen the potential income-tax blow.) The danger of not having a segregated growth portfolio is that an unexpected, and un-planned for, capital expense might reduce our retirement income permanently. The growth portion of the plan is often used to supplement one spouse's income after the passing of the other, since Social Security retirement benefits (and some pension payments) cease upon death. We'll talk more about estate planning later, but when it comes to blended families and avoiding long term enmity, the growth portion of your portfolio can be used in many creative ways to equalize estates and soothe unpleasant circumstances among heirs and beneficiaries.

Don't Speculate with Your Retirement Bins

The Bins and Gaps strategy of retirement planning helps us to segregate our savings dollars by putting our first five years of income into a conservative Bin that invests only in investment grade bonds, certificates of deposit, or other fixed investments. The annual interest earned during the first five years should help us to earn an increasing income that keeps pace with inflation, although significant spikes in inflation are something that will be problematic for anyone owning financial assets. As we mentioned, assets that traditionally have performed better over meaningful periods of time are used to fund our Bins that are set aside to be used in the future. Common stocks, for example, are subject to more vol-atility and should not be used in our immediate income Bin. Historically, however, they have proven to be a valuable asset class to hold in almost any portfolio. It's been my experience that an investor shouldn't buy a stock or a portfolio of stocks if he isn't prepared to commit to hold them for a meaningful period of time, which is perfect for later Bins. Day trading, options trading, and any other method that relies on your ability to outguess other speculators, including professionals and their computers, is more like fortune-telling than it is serious investing and has no place in a retirement portfolio that is designed to last the rest of your life.

I knew a man who had marginally enough assets to cover his lifetime gap and was living comfortably in a house that he had built and paid for. His son, who lived in his basement, took a course in commodities trading and convinced his father to let him manage the assets in his retirement account. Of course, the professional traders in Chicago, who ruthlessly trade commodities for a living, had their way with the amateur trader and the father was forced to sell his dream home and move to a rental unit in a senior community. It was a sad story and one that could've been avoided if someone had seriously explained how dangerous speculation can be. One of the reasons that I invented the Bins and Gaps strategy of retirement planning is that it helps to account for every dollar you can reasonably anticipate spending for the rest of your life.

If you have enough assets to comfortably cover your lifetime Gap, and you want to segregate assets from your Bins into a trading portfolio, that's entirely your call. But I wouldn't do that, and I would never recommend it, as losses you take in a trading account will have a direct effect on the income that you will need to survive. One of the benefits of the Bins and Gaps approach to retirement planning is that you segregate and invest enough money to fill your lifetime gap into Bins that are designed to support the lifestyle while any extra dollars can be used for other pursuits. I suggest that if you want to trade stocks, loan money to family members, or partake in any other pursuit that has a significant amount of uncertainty attached to it that you do that with dollars that are not part of your Funded Retirement. Anytime you deplete one of your Bins you risk the chance of now having a retirement that is "Unfunded."

Let's face it, the greatest uncertainty of planning for retirement is your life expectancy. None of us is promised tomorrow and planning to live to be 100 years old might seem overly hopeful when you're 65, but it seems more attainable as you turn 95. Replenishing your Bins and annually monitoring the growth (or lack of growth) of your portfolio is challenging as you get older; so we strongly recommend that you avoid speculation with any of the money in your Bins. That being said, there are some investments, for example real estate, that have traditionally done well over long periods of time, and they may be appropriate for a portion of your longer-term Bins. Income producing real estate, oil and gas royalties, and even stock dividends can all be included in your Bins, when appropriate. I will make an exception to my rule about putting only short-term and risk-free investments in my immediate Bin if you already own income producing assets such as these, but I make sure I have a backup plan in case this income suddenly ends.

Your Burn Rate

One of the calculations that I like to do is to annually figure out what percentage of assets, in total, we are spending to fill the annual gap. For example, if I have $1 million in my retirement plans and I am withdrawing $30,000 annually to fill my gap, then I know that I am burning money at the rate of 3% of my total assets. So, in theory, if my portfolio earns anything more than 3% I am increasing principal and if my annual investment return is below 3% I am depleting principal. In actuality, if I am using my Bin approach, I would calculate that my first five years' Bin holds $150,000, which is earning only short-term interest rates, so I'm actually interested to see if the remaining dollars in my portfolio ($850,000) is earning enough money to replace the dollars I am spending, which in this case means that my longer-term Bins need to average about 3.5%. This is a very useful calculation because if I am replenishing principal as fast as I spend it (or even faster) then I know that I can comfortably keep up with increases in the cost of living and also provide for my wife or me if I live to be older than 100.

Your Personal Cost-Of-Living Adjustment

One of the more interesting aspects of financial planning is that financial planning software allows us to enter any inflation rate that we judged to be reasonable as we create financial plans. It was a given, 25 years ago, that you calculated 3 ½ to 4% inflation in any financial projection that you made going forward. Today we live in times that are relatively inflation free, if not deflationary, and many financial planners have been using a calculation of only around 1% in their retirement plans. I prefer to look at an inflation rate that is based on your actual increases in your standard of living over the last year. While the government might use a complicated formula to calculate inflation in the economy, your personal rate of inflation is a little easier to figure out. For one thing, did you have money left over at the end of the first year? Is your rent going up? Is your health insurance going up? The best way to figure out your own inflation rate is by keeping a close eye on your retirement budget.

For the most part, it is safe to say that today's dollars will buy more than tomorrow dollars will, but just as the formative years of our careers were spent during the time of relatively high inflation (and relatively high interest rates), we are now facing a reality that includes lowering prices for goods and services and interest rates that are close to zero. I don't know if your personal cost of living will increase over time or not, so I recommend annual reviews and recalculations of your retirement budget to keep up with inflation. I've had retired clients tell me that inflation doesn't affect them at all; their house is paid for, the cars are paid for, and as they get older, they spend less money. You may have the same experience or you may not; a good retirement plan should anticipate any change in your cost of living.

Growth of Income

So how do you provide for increases in your monthly income? For one thing, your Social Security payments have a built-in cost-of-living adjustment. While in recent years this adjustment has been relatively meager; it is a calculation that is based upon the governments' estimation of inflation. Depending upon your personal cost-of-living increase, you can plan to increase your income based upon the performance of your longer-term Bins. As long as you are earning money at a higher rate than your burn rate you should be able to give yourself periodic raises. By "laddering" your short-term Bin, you should build an annual cost-of-living adjustment into your income as the interest pays upon the maturity of each short-term instrument. Your longer-term Bins can provide increases in income by investing in stocks that pay increasing dividends, inflation protected securities, or other assets that are designed to pay increasing rates of return.

The Loss of a Spouse

In a later chapter I'm going to talk more about estate planning and offer some solutions for the financial difficulties that accompany the loss of your spouse. I think it's important, however, to mention that it is a good idea to plan for the contingency of one of your Social Security payments (and perhaps one of your pension payments) going away upon the death of your life partner. Even though some of your expenses will drop, sometimes dramatically, when there is only one of you, the loss of Social Security income can make a significant difference in the size of your annual and lifetime Gap. One of the reasons that it is crucial that you remain a good steward of your retirement funds for all of your life is that your spouse may depend on those funds after you are gone. Maintaining the Bins and Gaps approach, with annual reviews, can help to protect those who are left behind.

It should be noted that most qualified retirement plans allow a surviving spouse to roll the deceased spouse's funds into an IRA in their own name with no immediate income tax consequences. This is not always the case with individually held annuities and some corporate pension plans, so a little preplanning is in order. And while I'm on the subject, let me urge you to check your beneficiaries, right now, on any retirement plans, life insurance policies, annuities, or IRA accounts that you have owned for more than a few years. It's a really bad day for the people you love if you have forgotten to change your beneficiary and your ex-spouse and her boy-friend inherit your retirement plan.

Income Taxes

One of the reasons that I recommend first using retirement accounts to fill your lifetime gap is that the proceeds that come from tax-deferred retirement accounts (except Roth IRAs) are taxed as regular income as they are withdrawn. By depleting these accounts over time we avoid a large tax bill if they are cashed in at the end of our lives. Other accounts, like Roth IRAs and stock portfolios that have large capital gains, are better left to our heirs because they have built-in tax advantages. Retirement accounts, on the other hand, are normally designed to be distributed over the course of our lifetime; in fact, when we reach 70 ½ years old we are required to take distributions based on our life expectancy. This is an event that requires planning.

When you reach 70 ½ years old you are forced to make a Required Minimum Distribution (RMD) from your retire-ment accounts that is based upon your age and the age of your beneficiary (if your beneficiary is your spouse). This amount usually starts off relatively small, somewhere around 3% of the value of your accounts on December 31 of the preceding year, and increases every year as you get older. The penalties for not making this withdrawal are severe: 50% of the amount you should have taken out is charged as a penalty; so it's a good idea to make sure that you have planned to withdraw from your retirement accounts as a part of your retirement plan. The amount that you withdraw is taxed as regular income, so if you have significant amounts of money in your retirement plans, it's probably a good idea to have your financial institution withhold income tax on these payments.

A full review of income taxes is beyond the scope of this book (and my expertise) but I would like to note that you may find yourself paying tax on half of your Social Security income, and even on your municipal bond interest (yes, your tax-free municipal bond interest) during retirement, so you may find that repositioning some of your non-retirement account assets into asset classes and investment vehicles that do not pay annual taxable income is a good strategy to minimize your taxation. Many baby boomers have placed most, if not all, of their assets in tax-deferred investments and may find themselves in a higher tax bracket in later retirement than was anticipated.

A strategy worth mentioning is called "the Roth conversion strategy" and it is something we look at for a client who retired during their 60s. Using our financial planning software; we calculate how much money we could take from a qualified retirement account (like an IRA rollover), pay income tax on it, and convert to a Roth IRA. We do this because the proceeds of a Roth IRA are never taxed, so we can establish a long-term growth account with no income tax due, a handy account to have later in retirement or to leave to our heirs. Because we are taking the money from our tax-deferred retirement accounts before we reach age 70 ½, our required minimum distributions (RMDs), when we reach that age, are based on a smaller account balance. Of course, the funds that you take out of your IRA are taxed as regular income, so we tend to not do this for someone who has a high-paying job well into their late 60s. And if we wait until after you are 70 ½, we have to take required minimum distribution before we take money out for your Roth IRA, and we can't use that RMD to fund a Roth conversion. So you have to take one distribution for your RMD, and then make another one for your Roth conversion, which rarely makes good sense. However; this powerful strategy is very useful when the situation is right. We often find that money we set aside from a Roth conversion is perfectly suited for funding our longest term Bin.

Why Not Annuitize?

One of the benefits of funding your own retirement is that you have options that weren't available to you if you only had the option of receiving a fixed pension. While a pension is a dependable source of income for the rest of your life, it lacks flexibility. If the idea of having a dependable, guaranteed paycheck for the rest of your life appeals to you, you can, right now, use your retirement plan assets to purchase an immediate annuity that will give you all of the benefits of a traditional pension plan. I'm not against it. In fact, your employer may give you the option to receive pension payments or a lump sum payment, and only you can decide which you prefer. Your decision depends upon your comfort level with managing your own money versus the security of knowing that you will have a lifetime income. Comfort level is very, very important and some people will gladly trade the uncertainty that comes with collecting a lifetime income from their retirement assets versus receiving one from a guaranteed source, like a pension or annuity. In truth, if you use my formula and determined that you have a fully Funded Retirement, you have essentially created your own annuity, although you are assuming the risk that might be passed on to the insurance company. If you successfully manage the funds to provide income, growth of income, and growth of principal, you can achieve many of the benefits of an annuity contract without giving up all of your principal.

Even if your company does not offer you the lifetime income option, you can always shop around various insurance companies to price a lifetime annuity. These annuities can be purchased within your retirement plan, so that you are taxed only as you receive payments, and provisions can be made so that your spouse can continue to receive full or partial payments after your death. Keep in mind, the factors used to calculate your monthly payments are the anticipated interest rates the insurance company will earn on your funds and your life expectancy. An annuity is basically the opposite of a life insurance policy, which insures against an early death, an annuity insures against outliving your principal. Some companies will take into account your health, and if you have had health problems they might pay a higher monthly check.

I think that fixed annuities have a place in many retirement portfolios. Think of them as an option that is always there for you if you decide to purchase one. If you actually annuitize all of your retirement assets you have permanently traded your money for an anticipated lifetime income. The concept of leaving a large lump sum to your heirs is reduced by the amount of money you send to the insurance company. And unless your annuity has a cost of living rider built in (which costs money), you will not receive cost-of-living adjustments to your income.

There are some annuity contracts that have new features that will pay a lifetime income to you without you surrendering all of your funds to the insurance company. They have a guaranteed rate of withdrawal as you spend your own principal that will continue after you have used all of your money: an income that you can't outlive. If you die before you have depleted all of your assets, a lump sum is paid to your heirs. These annuities can be an effective retirement planning tool; in the right circumstances. But I'd like to get on my soapbox, and suggest that no investment, no matter what it is, is a solution to everyone's problems, and despite the free lunch seminars you probably get invited to once a week (I get an invitation delivered to my home at least that frequently), an annuity is not the answer to every retirement question that you have.

If you are the type of person who is confident that your cost of living will not increase dramatically and who relies on a monthly check to fill your lifetime Gap, I think annuitizing some or all of your funds should be on your radar. If your employer gives you the opportunity to annuitize your funds I would compare that option to other immediate annuities that may be available to you (usually your employer gets the best rate from the insurance company). If you have a fully Funded Retirement and purchase an annuity, you have traded your retirement account assets for a "paid in full" retirement. That trade may or may not be something that you can live with, and I often find that annuitizing a portion of your retirement assets is a good solution to filling your Gap.

If you have annuitized payments coming in each month, you calculate those payments as part of your Base income along with your Social Security and any other pension payments you may have. You might think of annuitized payments as your personal pension plan. If you have enough money in your retirement plans to consider your retirement fully

Funded then you should be able to purchase an annuity that adequately fills your lifetime Gap. If not, I don't see the point. One of the benefits of using the Bins and Gaps method of retirement planning is that you have conservatively estimated your retirement needs, and whether an insurance company pays you to fill your Gap, or you fill it through your own managed money, is not material; you have enough funds either way. As part of my decision I would also consider the fact that if interest rates go higher, and as I get older, I may be able to earn a higher monthly payment from an annuity. In the meantime, partially funding my gap with an annuity payment is reasonable and sometimes advisable. I like the concept of retaining flexibility and having the ability to give myself periodic raises or cover major expenses without interrupting my income stream. Annuitizing all of your retirement assets is an extreme step and you should examine all your options before you sign the papers!

The Overfunded Retirement

I've met many people who don't have a gap at all when it comes to their retirement funding. Pension and Social Security income cover all of their living expenses, and they don't plan to ever touch their retirement assets. I know other people who have many more assets in the retirement accounts than they need to fund their retirement. It's been my experience that these people got this way because they are pretty good with money, and they're not going to change how they handle it simply because they retired. The Bins and Gaps approach to retirement planning is still useful to these folks—forcing yourself to look at part of your funds as longer term assets is a great discipline for any investor. Good stewardship of retirement assets, for them, becomes an issue of protecting assets, good tax planning, and setting assets aside funds for their heirs.

Saying that retirement is overfunded is sort of like saying that you have too much money, or that you're in too good a shape, or that you have eaten too much pizza: it's a matter of judgment. If you need a relatively small amount of income from your retirement assets to fill your gap, I still recommend going through the exercise of putting enough assets in your lifetime Bins. As life changes come along, and as you begin to face your Required Minimum Distributions and estate planning decisions a disciplined approach to investing can only work in your favor.

The Bins and Gaps approach to retirement financing is not simply designed to generate income, it is also a model that enforces discipline on investors and helps them to maintain a long-term approach to money management. If you eliminate the need for immediate income, your first Bin simply becomes money that you have the option to spend or not spend in the first five years of retirement. If you truly don't need the money, and don't come up with something to do with it, you can simply roll the money into a Bin designed for a longer-term investment as it comes due. As you reach the age where you have to take a required minimum distribution (RMD), you can withdraw money from your Bins to meet these distributions.

Bumps in the Road

"The best laid schemes o' mice an' men / Gang aft a-gley." Robert Burns

Things go wrong. No matter how carefully we plan, we are subject to the whims of life. Whether it's a health crisis, a hurricane that blows the roof off our house, or a financial market that makes us wish we had hidden our money in our mattress; our plans can go awry. The reason I urge retirees to invest a portion of their funds with an eye towards growth is to help make it through bad situations. If you can cover large capital expenses without depleting the money that is generating your income, you are more likely to survive a storm. And if you have taken a long-term approach to investing and covered your Gaps, some storms will be easier to get through than others.

If you have a Funded Retirement but make bad investment decisions or bad budgeting decisions, you may find yourself quickly falling into the "Unfunded" retirement category. And if you should have to withdraw a significant amount of principal from your assets, you also run the risk of becoming Unfunded. The discipline required to maintain a Funded Retirement requires that you are not invading, unless it is from the planned spending, of your current Bin.

In 2008, during the financial crisis, no matter how diversified you were, if you owned any kind of financial asset you felt some pain. So much money left the system so quickly that investors were indiscriminately selling good and bad assets. Retirees who had their immediate income needs covered for several years, like in the first Bin, were able to weather the storm easier than those who were relying on all of their assets to generate an immediate income. In a future chapter I'm going to talk about the risks of investing in a rising interest rate environment and how you can plan to avoid the inevitable storm of rising interest rates and their effects on your portfolio. And while diversifying is a much discussed topic among financial planners, if you only own financial assets that are subject to stock and bond market fluctuations you are not as diversified as you might think, complete diversification includes assets other than stocks and bonds.

If you have not been able to set money aside for unexpected expenses during retirement, or if you have simply decided to collect an annuity (or pension) check for the rest of your life, an emergency that requires cash may not be something that you can solve easily. The reason that we consider "growth" one of the important legs of our investment stool is that there probably will come a time during your retirement when cash is needed. We've already talked about planning to fund a widow or widower's retirement to make up for the gap in the loss of one's Social Security payments—a perfect example of the kind of bump in the road that we will all face at some point. For those who approach retirement without a budget and without the discipline of the Bins and Gaps approach to retirement planning, an unexpected financial emergency might be catastrophic.

Long-Term Care

There is nothing that accelerates the burn rate of your retirement portfolio like the necessity of long-term care such as a nursing home or other type of medical care. No matter how many assets you set aside, if you end up in a situation where you or your spouse requires extensive healthcare you might run out of money. I hate to be so blunt, but I've seen it happen. While purchasing long-term care insurance may seem like an unnecessary expense, it is often the best way to protect your retirement assets over the course of your lifetime. If you consider the cost of long-term care insurance as a percentage of your total assets it becomes clear that this type of protection is worth the annual premium. In a later chapter I talk a lot about comprehensive retirement planning and about looking at your retirement plan in a holistic manner. You can bet that long-term care insurance is a reasonable option for many retirees.

The care and feeding of a Funded Retirement portfolio is relatively simple compared to the diligence needed to retire Unfunded. We'll talk about that next.

8

THE UNFUNDED RETIREMENT

**Caught between the longing for love
And the struggle for the legal tender...
Jackson Browne**

**401(k)/IRA Balances for Median Working Households
with a 401(k), Age 55-64, by Income Quintile, 2013**

Income range (quintiles)	Median 401(k)/IRA balance	Percent with 401(k)
Less than $39,000	$13,000	22%
$39,000-60,999	53,000	48
$61,000-90,999	100,000	60
$91,000-137,999	132,000	65
$138,000 or more	452,000	68
Total	**111,000**	**52**

Source: Center for Retirement Research at Boston College calculations from U.S. Board of Governors of the Federal Reserve System. Survey of Consumer Finances, 2013.

Welcome to a judgment free zone! This may be the only financial book that you are ever going to read that doesn't try to make you feel bad about not having set aside enough funds for retirement. I get it. Saving for retirement is hard; just look at the numbers above! That being said, I'm not going to spend this chapter telling you to "hope for the Best," or "live your life as if money wasn't an issue." Money is always an issue, and this is, after all, a book about financial planning. So, let's have a serious, realistic, and friendly chat about retiring without enough assets to fill your Lifetime Gap.

I define a Funded Retirement as one in which you have enough assets in your retirement accounts to cover your lifetime gap in today's dollars. As an example, if your projected retirement budget is $2000 a month and you have $1600 a month coming in from Social Security and you are 65 years old: multiply your $400 a month deficit times 12 to get an annual gap of $4800. We multiply $4800 times 35 years (to get you to age 100) for a lifetime gap of $168,000. If your retirement account balance is greater than $168,000 we consider your retirement to be Funded, and your primary job is to keep up with inflation, preserve principle, and have dollars set aside for unexpected (or expected) large capital expenses. Like a lot of financial decisions, I recommend that you do some calculations and let the numbers guide you before you make any emotional decisions from which you can't financially recover.

EXAMPLE: CALCULATING A FUNDED RETIREMENT

Projected retirement budget:	$2,000 per month
Projected Social Security income:	- $1,600 per month
Gap:	$400 per month
	x 12 months
Annual Gap:	$4,800
	x 35 years*
Lifetime Gap:	$168,000

*Assuming for this example that you are 65 years old, multiply the annual gap by 35 to get you to age 100 for your lifetime gap.

For this example, a retirement balance of
$168,000 or more
would be considered a funded retirement.

If you don't have enough funds in your retirement account to cover your Lifetime Gap then you are leaving *something* up to chance. You are either hoping that you can lower your monthly budget or that your investments will perform well enough to make up for your deficit. Given the choice of the two, I'd rather see you try to make some hard choices to lower your Projected Retirement Budget; putting too much pressure on your portfolio performance, as we shall see, is no way to approach retirement. There is a third option: to base the calculation of your Lifetime Gap on an age younger than 100, and I honestly believe that, while this approach might make the numbers work, it is the opposite of good retirement planning. I have never said this to a client, "Well, Grandma, as long as you die around age 75, your retirement plan is just fine." Marrying a rich widow, winning the lottery, and letting your kids support you are also options that fall outside the realm of retirement planning; they can all happen, but I'm not qualified to advise you on them! I believe you can find YouTube videos on all of these topics.

Your Burn Rate

I usually only recommend that you only consider retirement when it is Funded; the practice of trying to sustain a lifestyle from which you did not have the appropriate savings is more risky than any reasonable retiree should be expected to bear. If you do not have enough assets in your retirement accounts to cover your current lifetime gap, in today's dollars, then I suggest that the first thing you do is figure out how many years your current retirement assets are funding. For example, if you have a $3000 annual gap and $36,000 in your retirement accounts then you have 12 years of assets on hand; if you are 65 years old you have enough money to last until you are 77. At 77, I'm fairly certain that you will find it difficult to reenter the job market. If your assets last well into your 90s, then you may feel more comfortable retiring now, with the knowledge that you need to either adjust your budget or increase your investment return during your retirement. Keep in mind that we plan to spend down principal in even a Funded Retirement, we hope to make up for what we spend through the performance of our investments. If you are spending relatively small amounts of principal, it is easier to recoup the dollars you are spending to support your lifestyle. An Unfunded Retirement requires that you spend significant amounts of principal to maintain your lifestyle.

Having an open and honest relationship with your budget numbers is the only way to avoid disaster in your retirement years. There are many retirees, as the chart above demonstrates, who will not have successfully saved enough money to fund their retirement; yet many of them live happy and fulfilling lives by keeping a part time job or adjusting to a lower retirement budget. There's no shame in that; forgive me, but I think there is shame in not taking the time to understand your finances and making lifelong decisions without the proper preparation. The worst thing a professional advisor can do is tell you that you have saved enough money for retirement when you haven't, so I'm going to be fairly plain spoken here. Running out of assets in your old age is a terrible thing, and if you embark on a retirement journey with a lifestyle that is too ambitious for your budget you are going to eventually run out of money.

If you do not have a Funded Retirement then you need to do this next set of calculations to determine how serious your deficit is. The first thing I want to know is, at current anticipated spending rates, how long will my money last? This is a pretty easy calculation; all you have to do is divide your annual deficit into your current account balance. For example, if you have a $1000 monthly deficit, that's $12,000 annually and if your account balance is $100,000 then you have 8.3 years of living expenses on hand. Now, if we add 8.3 years to your current age (in this example you are 65 years old), you know that you have enough assets on hand to last until you are a little over 73 years old.

The next number I want to know is: how much do my assets have to earn annually to replenish the principle I'm spending each year? Again, using our example, if I have $100,000 and withdraw $12,000, I'm left with $88,000. With that $88,000 left, how much does my portfolio have to earn each year to get back to my original $100,000 of principle? The simple math tells me to divide $12,000 by $88,000, and I will reach this number: 13.63%. That's a pretty scary number to me, even as a professional investment advisor; I would hate to think that my survival depends upon the financial markets returning that high an annual return during every year of my retirement. To make it worse, thanks to inflation and my need to give myself cost-of-living adjustments, I need to add an even higher return to compensate for inflation. And if I have an unexpected major expense, I am in really big trouble.

If I ever have a year where I do not meet my required rate of return my efforts become even tougher the following year: let's say that in year one I spend $12,000 and only recoup $6000 in my portfolio (which represents a 6.81% return) and begin the next year withdrawing my $12,000 in expenses from my new principal amount of $94,000. Now, to get back to $94,000 my portfolio would have to return 14.63% (12,000÷82,000), and to return to my original principal amount of $100,000 my portfolio will have to have a one-year performance of 21.95%! Look, there is no professional investment manager who would willingly take on those numbers, why should you?

Just ask the United States government, who has the distinct advantage of being able to print money, about deficit spending, and you can see why going into retirement without enough assets to fill your lifetime gap is fraught with peril. Unlike the government, you won't have the opportunity to spend your way out of the deficit. Before you put too much pressure on your portfolio advisor, I suggest that if you think it's easy to earn high returns like 14.63% or even 21.95% on your investment dollars that you do it now, before you retire, while you still have an opportunity to replace any losses that you may take from the extra risks you will have to incur to achieve such high returns.

And we aren't even talking about years that have negative returns, when you are spending principle and losing principle at the same time. Let's assume that after I withdraw $12,000 from the $84,000 I started the year with, my portfolio runs into a bear market in the following year. After a 10% loss, I begin the year with $73,200 in my account. After withdrawing my $12,000 for that year, I now realize that I am down to a little over five years of assets left in my retirement account when my balance is down to $61,200. Getting back to my original principal value of $100,000 seems like a dream now and I am forced to consider major lifestyle changes before my assets are all the way down to zero.

What Are My Options?

If you do not have enough dollars set aside in your retirement accounts, you are, in one way or another, assuming some risk if you decide to retire right now. The risk is either approaching the later years of your retirement without enough funds to maintain your lifestyle, or being forced to invest in a manner that forces you to assume more risk then you should. When you think about it you only have three choices if you are retirement is Unfunded:

1. You can adjust your Anticipated Retirement Budget.

2. You can attempt to increase investment return (and assume more investment risk) to fill your gap.

3. You can defer retirement.

Almost every survey of baby boomers who are considering retirement says that the majority of them are concerned that they do not have enough assets to retire. Part of this is due to uncertainty about the performance of their investments, and part of this is due to the fact that many of us have not been able to save enough money to support our chosen lifestyle in retirement. I hope that the formulas I've given you so far in this book have helped you to decide if you have enough assets set aside for retirement or not. The Bins and Gaps method of retirement planning should help you to understand if you have enough money set aside for retirement and your money management priorities.

Your Projected Retirement Budget

One of the hardest things for me, personally, is to live to a budget. I absolutely hate the entire process of writing down every nickel I spend, anticipating all of my planned expenses, and keeping my charge cards in my pocket. I get away with my relatively undisciplined lifestyle because I am still working, I'm fortunate enough to have a successful business, and I know that I can dig my way out of any hole I create for myself. I am painfully aware that once I retire, I will have to learn to avoid the impulse part of impulse spending. So believe me, I understand how reluctant you may be to prepare a projected retirement budget. I'm afraid that you have no option but to suck it up, get out the yellow legal pad, and start keeping track of your expenses.

Should I Pay off Debt?

Any retirement guide that you read is going to suggest that you pay off your credit cards and any other revolving debt before you retire. If you find, at this point in your life, that you can't do that, then I suggest you pick up Dave Ramsey's book, *Total Money Makeover*. It has some brilliant methods to help you emerge from debt. If you don't think want to focus on paying off debt, then I would make sure that you include monthly credit card payments in your projected budget for any current payments that you have and any purchases that you plan on making.

Likewise, I have always felt that I would rather make car payments on a newer car than own an older car that requires expensive maintenance. But lately I've been enjoying the concept of no car payments at all, even if I have to buy tires and brakes, now and then. Whether you have payments due on your vehicles or you have regular maintenance to anticipate, car expenses should be included in your projected retirement budget. In other words, in drafting your projected retirement budget it is crucial that you try to anticipate all of your expenses. Your projected budget is the cornerstone to having a financially successful retirement and any omission will cause you to make adjustments going forward.

I'd like you to keep in mind one more thing: any dollars that you withdraw from your retirement plan are taxable, so it is really advisable to pay off significant balances, like cars or mortgages, from your non-retirement assets before you decide to retire. If you pull a large amount of money from your retirement plan to pay off your cars, or even your mortgage, you should understand that you may kick yourself into a higher tax bracket, and this is an especially bad idea to do this during your last calendar year of work. If, after doing the appropriate calculations, you decide that you have enough surplus in your retirement accounts to pay off large balances, it is often best to do so after January 1 of your first retirement year, so that your withdrawal is not added to the income you received while working. It's quite a dilemma for retirees with relatively small retirement account balances to decide whether they should deplete their retirement accounts to pay off debt or try to manage the debt during retirement.

Sometimes you may decide to carry your car payment for one or two years of retirement, until it's paid off, and then adjust your retirement budget later. Likewise, with a mortgage, if you only have a few years of payments left, it might be best to carry your mortgage for a few years and then adjust your lifetime gap downward after you've had your mortgage burning party. Flexibility is one of the strengths of the Bins and Gaps method of retirement planning, and if you want to do a little extra math you can adjust your lifetime gap downwards or upwards if you know that you will soon have major debts paid off. All that being said, if your original calculations show that your funds are sufficient to last until your mid-90s then you're probably able to carry some relatively short-term debt into the first few years of retirement. However, if your original calculations show that you could run out of money in your 80s or even your late 70s; I might reevaluate my decision to retire right now.

Being a numbers oriented kind of guy, I like to get out my business calculator, a yellow legal pad, and my computer to calculate the actual cost of carrying debt versus making taxable withdrawals from my retirement accounts to pay off debt now. In that calculation I want to consider the opportunity I've lost by not having those funds to invest in my retirement account, the taxes I'll have to pay, and compare that to the cost of paying debt off over time. Like a lot of financial decisions, seeing your particular numbers in black and white is the only way to make a decision, and a good Comprehensive Retirement Plan should include this calculation.

One of the things that almost never works is borrowing your way into retirement. Home equity loans can be useful, or deadly, depending upon the method in which they are used. During the housing boom I ran into a number of people who were *"taking"* the cash out of their house. I wondered, to myself (and to them; sometimes I can't keep my mouth shut), if they were selling off pieces of the house a little bit at a time to raise cash or if they were actually *"borrowing"* the cash out of their house. A lot of these people, sometimes at the advice of financial professionals, were borrowing the equity in their homes and investing the money in stocks (there was radio show here in Orlando that advocated this approach). When the real estate market collapsed, you guessed it, so did their equity portfolio, and some of these folks were forced to cash in their stocks at the bottom of the market to re-pay their home equity loans. While I don't advocate withdrawing money from your retirement account to pay off your mortgage in a lump sum, I sure don't advocate borrowing money and putting your home at risk to fund your retirement. This is especially true of what I think is the next great financial crisis: the reverse mortgage boondoggle that is being propagated upon seniors throughout our country.

Adjusting your projected retirement budget lower can be a simple matter of lowering expectations, or it may require significant changes in your projected retirement lifestyle. Some of us look forward to the concept of simplifying our lives and slowing down the pace of our spending; some of us won't have any choice in the matter. Depending upon the size of your lifetime gap you may find that you and your family may have to have serious discussions about some lifestyle changes that will allow you to retire now.

The Mercy of the Markets

Even if you have a Funded Retirement it is still important to earn a return that at least keeps up with inflation and, hopefully, at a rate that replenishes the money you are spending during each retirement year. Simply accomplishing these tasks requires a decent amount of investment acumen. If you are burning cash at a rate faster than you are spending it, by definition, you are depleting assets. If you are approaching retirement without the proper funding to cover your lifetime gap, then you are having to assume risk and take chances in your portfolio. Sooner or later this will catch up with you.

In investing there is a term called the "risk-free rate," the interest rate currently paid by short-term U.S. Treasury Bills, and it implies that we will get 100% of our principal returned and earn an interest rate that pays us for the use of our money and the inflation we were exposed to while we loan our money to the government. Currently, as I write this book in early 2015, the 91 day T-bill is paying about 0.015%—close to zero. Any investment return, then, that pays more than the risk-free rate, by definition has risk built into it. If I buy a five-year government bond, for example, I may not be risking my principal, since I'm loaning my money to the government, but I am running the risk that interest rates will go higher during the five years I own the bond. If I loan my money to a company with a low credit rating and buy what is called a "junk-bond" for five years, I should not only be compensated for the inflation over those five years and the possibility that interest may go higher, but also for the fact that my principal is now at risk. All investments have some measure of risk, and it is up to you, the investor, to identify what risks you are willing to assume and which you are not.

We are currently in an environment in which savers are forced into becoming investors, and they are being forced to assume more risk than they may realize they have bought into. Let this grizzled old veteran tell you, Wall Street is not a warm or fuzzy place. Investing is not for the faint of heart, and retirees who are asking their portfolios to outperform the professionals in the investment community are asking a lot of themselves. Professional investment firms close their doors all the time after making bad bets; no amount of education or talent can save you if you are on the wrong side of the financial markets. Trying to make up for a deficit in your retirement savings by out-guessing Wall Street is a sucker's bet, and if you have any say in the matter I would rather see you defer retirement for a few years than attempt to retire only to be forced to return to the workforce.

In a later chapter, I'm going to talk about the risks of investing in an increasing interest rate environment. Should you currently own bonds, in particular, you will watch your principal decline significantly in value if interest rates return to higher levels. If you invest your first few years of income in assets that are exposed to the fluctuations of the stock and bond markets you may find that you are unable to meet your income needs; that's why I recommend placing your first five years of income (your first Bin) in savings vehicles like government bonds, money markets, and certificates of deposit. Over longer and more meaningful periods of time, financial investments usually do well, but there have been prolonged periods of time where there is little or no return in the stock market (see the 1970s or 1930s). No retirement plan should depend upon your ability to accurately predict the short-term returns of the financial markets.

The Risk Menu

I think it's a very good idea to understand some of the more common types of risk that you will encounter as an investor. This is by no means an all-inclusive list, just some of the more common types of risk that you assume if you buy financial assets, and, as you read through these, try to see which ones apply to your current investments and if you can live with the risks that I'm describing.

1.) Principle Risk: if I loan money to the kid named Bill who is messing around with computers in the garage next door, I may or may not get my money back. If you give him capital in exchange for a piece of his business we call that "equity." When you own a stock you have essentially purchased shares in a company with no guarantee that you will ever have your principal returned; you could only hope that someone will come along and buy the shares from you. If the kid next door was named Bill Gates, someone probably did offer to buy your shares, and, with any luck, you are wealthy because you believed in him! If the kid next door wasn't quite as successful, you may have lost your investment.

2.) Credit Risk: if you purchase a bond you are subject to credit risk; bonds are nothing more than loans. The US government is one of the few borrowers who is said to have no credit risk it all; almost all other bonds are subject to some degree of credit risk, and independent rating agencies rate the bonds accordingly. Higher rated bonds have very little credit risk, but Wall Street is littered with the bodies of formerly high-rated companies who couldn't pay off their bonds. Junk bonds, which were probably never highly rated to begin with, pay a very high interest rate because they have to; it's the only way they can lure investment dollars to offset the high credit risk.

3.) Opportunity Risk: one of the more significant problems that baby boomers face as they head towards retirement is the fact that many of them have been too conservative with their investments, leaving their 401(k) balances in cash equivalents like money markets and low paying fixed accounts. They lost the opportunity to have their money grow, and we investment type guys like to warn you that almost any time you use money for something other than investment it might be said that you have assumed opportunity risk. There are legends of $200,000 snowmobiles that were purchased in the state of Washington by Microsoft employees who cashed in their first stock options and bought snowmobiles. By not owning Microsoft stock when it went up, and instead cashing in their options, they lost the opportunity to watch their funds grow. The stock options they used to buy those snowmobiles grew to ridiculously high prices.

4.) Currency Risk: global investment is all the rage now, but if you invest in a country whose currency goes down significantly in value you will eventually need to pay more for the dollars you repatriate when your money comes back home. Anytime you invest in a market other than ones that use U.S. dollars, you are subject to currency risk. It might even be said that you assume currency risk while you own dollars, since inflation cuts into your purchasing power and erodes the value of your dollars over time.

5.) Political Risk: just as there is risk in currency, your foreign investments might be subject to a coup or nationalization of your assets. If a foreign government decides to seize the investments of a company that you are investing in, you have been the victim of political risk.

6.) Interest Rate Risk: if you own a bond that is paying a 5% rate of return, and interest rates go higher, and comparable bonds now pay 7%, the market value of your bond will go down. Think about it: why would I buy your 5% Bond when I can go get a 7% bond? The only way I would is if I got a cheaper price on your bond. (A later chapter will go into interest rate risk in more detail.)

7.) Liquidity Risk: we take it for granted that there will always be someone there to buy our securities at the exact date and time that we are ready to sell, but that is not always the case. Some securities do not trade regularly, and in certain market conditions, buyers may be hard to find for all securities. We especially notice this with very low priced securities, called Penny Stocks, which only trade infrequently, so the seller of a penny stock might not find a buyer when he is ready to cash out. But liquidity risk is not limited to just penny stocks, in certain market conditions even the bluest of blue chip stocks might see its trading imbalanced or even halted. After the tragic events of 9/11 the financial markets were closed for a week, and no one was able to sell their stocks.

8.) Systematic Risk: the risk inherent owning any financial assets. Normally, we can trust the financial system, but there have been periods where everything, no matter what classification of assets, goes down in value (see 2008 financial crisis). When the entire system is in turmoil even good, solid companies can be subject to extreme drops in value.

My point in describing the various forms of risk is not to frighten you, but to have a good, grownup talk about the realities of investing. While some risks are more frightening than others to the retiree, we should always be aware of the benefits and the consequences of each and every financial decision. The Bins and Gaps approach to retirement planning helps to reduce your short term exposure to risk while allowing you to take a longer term view of the investments you won't be needing for a little while.

Reverse Engineer It

If you are tremendously Unfunded and at wits end about your job, yet you still have some flexibility in your retirement plans, it isn't a bad idea to divide your retirement plan balance by the number of years until you are 100 years old to arrive at a relatively safe withdrawal rate. For example: if you have a retirement balance of $100,000 and you are 67 years old, it's probably safe to begin to withdraw $3,000 a year, or $250 a month from your retirement plan, with annual increases for cost of living adjustments. Of course, I strongly recommend the systematic and disciplined approach to investing that is the Bins and Gaps approach.

The alternatives—spending too much principal or assuming too much risk—are both relatively short term behaviors that will eventually catch up with you. If you are able to budget within your base income and can withstand waiting to take an income from your retirement accounts, you might consider skipping the first five year Bin and move all your money (except a contingency fund) into your second Bin. Leaving your principle intact for 5 years gives it the opportunity for all 100% of it to grow (since you aren't taking withdrawals), and your years to age 100 are lessened by five years.

As an example: Joe has $100,000 in his retirement account at age 65, and rather than draw from it, he decides to supplement his income with a part-time job at the local bike shop. When he turns 70 he is happy to see that his account, which earned a hypothetical 6% a year, is now worth $126,248 and divided by his 30 years to age 100 equals a $350 monthly payment. At this point in his life Joe can now begin to withdraw from his second Bin and manage his money with an eye towards all of the methods associated with the Bins and Gaps method.

Hypothetical Illustrations and Real Expectations

Let me talk a little bit about this last example and the hypothetical 6% figure that I used. Why, you might wonder, didn't Joe just follow his stockbroker's advice and simply withdraw $500 a month (that's what 6% on $100,000 pays) and hope to leave his principal intact because of high hoped-for investment returns. That's sort of why I've written this book for you, because times have changed, and if you base your retirement income on *almost any* hypothetical figure you are exposing yourself to some form of risk. There is, quite simply, no easy way to earn a current rate of 6% and while you might hope that a 6% return is realistic, you just don't know. I picked the number for this example because it *has* been a reasonable investment return for a blended portfolio, historically. Of course I know this in hindsight. The trouble is, we just don't have any way to lock in a good rate at this point in history, and it is more prudent to withdraw funds based on life expectancy. I'd rather get good performance, like a 6% return, and make annual adjustments based on actual investment results as opposed to hypothetical returns.

I like the concept of five year Bins because it gives us a reasonable period of time to let the market move in long-term, definitive trends.

As I've illustrated earlier in this chapter, trying to fund your retirement deficit by assuming a non-guaranteed rate of withdrawal is dangerous. I've seen people who are paying themselves a fixed monthly income from their retirement account, year after year, without adjustment for market performance or inflation. This works for as long as markets are going higher but can become irreversible in bad markets. No matter how positive or enthusiastic you are about the stock market's future performance, the market doesn't care. The market doesn't care when you bought in or where you plan to get out, and while I, myself, am an optimistic long-term stock investor, I certainly cannot guarantee you that the market has not already reached its long term high. Prudent financial planning tells us keep the current interest rate environment in mind. When interest rates go higher I will certainly revise my current expectations for withdrawing from retirement accounts.

Deferring Retirement

This alternative of deferring retirement is very popular right now; a lot of Baby Boomers are choosing to remain in the workforce. The advantages are evident; you are probably in your peak earning years, by delaying Social Security you get to earn a larger monthly check, and if you are using the Bins and Gaps method of retirement planning, you have a smaller number to use when you divide your retirement account balance by the number of years until you reach 100 years old. In addition, you have more years to contribute to your retirement plan. Given the current state of the investment world, you can't blame someone who decides to defer retirement a few years.

Let's look at our friend Joe, from the last example. At age 65 he had $100,000 in his retirement account and decided to continue his corporate job. He was able to add $10,000 a year to his retirement account with his company match, so his account, which still grew at 6% was now worth $172,618 with his new contributions. Based on his 30 year life expectancy, he can safely withdraw $480 a month from his retirement accounts before his annual adjustments. Since Joe waited until he was 70 years old to withdraw his Social Security, he will receive a 32% larger check than he would have if he collected at his full retirement age of 66! He also paid the balance on his mortgage down by making extra payments during these five years. Since circumstances had prevented Joe from accumulating many assets before he reached age 65, deferring retirement proved to be a financially sound decision.

Deciding to defer retirement is viewed by some as an act of penance for not saving enough, as a labor to be endured by others, and as a great opportunity by still others. Once you get laser focused on something as important as retirement, it is amazing how you can make things happen. Of course, no one is promised tomorrow, and you have to weigh the quality of your life if you retire early vs. deferring until a later age; I am pretty sure that your daily happiness should count as much as your financial well- being.

Trapped

Here's the nightmare: a potential retiree is locked into a house that they can't sell at a high enough price to get their mortgage paid off, they have no retirement savings, and they are down-sized from their job. God bless! There is a lot of this going around, and we can all strive to avoid this situation, because, honestly, there aren't a lot of good answers. This situation is closer to poverty than the result of successful retirement planning, and at this point a bankruptcy lawyer is probably the only guy with a reasonable solution. But what can we learn from this scenario?

For one thing, we can come to the realization that a retirement lifestyle has two components: the income and the expenditures. Even those of us who have saved a reasonable amount of money for retirement need to come to the understanding that our Projected Retirement Budget is the result of our choices and we can best control our retirement lifestyle by making smart financial decisions about our expenses. Do we still need a brand new car? Do we still need such a large house? Can we find ways to occupy our time that don't cost a lot of money? Even retirees with the smallest retirement accounts can live happy retirements if they design a retirement lifestyle that allows them to live within their means. Retirement, after all, should be about leaving the rat race behind and living a comfortable and happy life. Consumerism is a particularly American habit, and, like most habits, it's one we can learn to break.

9

WHEN INTEREST RATES GO HIGHER

But what a fool believes he sees
No wise man has the power to reason away
What seems to be
Is always better than nothing.
Kenny Loggins

"Only a fool tries to predict interest rates
or the stock market."
Wall St. Maxim

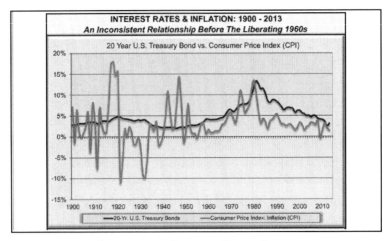

Source: www.CrestmontResearch.com

In this chapter I'd like to try to place today's low interest rates in historical perspective, talk about some of the special risks associated with investing in a rising interest rate environment, and, finally, talk about why I think investing in the asset class of equities is a reasonable choice for your longer-term Bins. While on the subject, I want to talk a little about the difference between being an investor and being a speculator. Portfolio selection is dependent upon many things, including current market conditions, your risk tolerance, and no small amount of research. The ever-green nature of this type of book means that investment ideas that seem logical as I write this chapter might not be appropriate in the future (including this afternoon). When implementing a portfolio for my clients, I certainly have particular assets and asset classes that I favor; but I can tell you that no two clients' portfolios are identical! I leave the investment selection to you, or you and your investment professional. I hope that this chapter serves as some sort of framework to help with your decisions. The primary message I have for you is to stay flexible and not to get locked into any one investment scenario that involves making big bets on the direction of interest rates.

I tell a story to bore my clients every once in a while. When I was a new stockbroker, one of my closest family members opened an account with me to trade stock options. This was before the internet, so he would call once or twice a day, every day, trying to outmaneuver the Wall Street traders. He would ask me, every day, what I thought would happen next in the markets, like in the next few minutes. The stress of these conversations was killing me; this guy, whom I love, was never terribly interested in my ability to predict the future before, but now he was hoping I was an oracle. I was not.

Today; after many years of experience, I have come to the conclusion that anyone who thinks that they can accurately predict the future behavior of markets is either delusional, lucky, or a little of both. Those market traders (or speculators) remind me of everyone I know who goes to Las Vegas and comes home saying, "we broke even." Nope! Those casinos make money somehow and I'm pretty sure it's because most people lose when they go to Vegas. Trying to outguess the professional traders, money managers, and computer trading programs is an exercise in probability: sooner or later you are going to lose too. I believe that retirees have a better chance of investing successfully by taking a long-term value oriented approach.

So, the question is: why would you build a retirement portfolio based on assumptions that might not turn out to be true? When dealing with any money, but especially retirement assets, it is best to have the flexibility and awareness to react to current conditions without going too far out on any particular limb. Since we are now living an environment of historically low interest rates, it is easy to assume that they will one day go higher. But when? Wall St. types have been calling for higher interest rates for a few years now and they have been wrong. It's worth remembering that even a stopped clock is right twice a day. So eventually rates will go higher and a rising interest rate environment causes a particularly excruciating kind of pain.

Do you remember when your grandparents bragged about earning 13% on their certificates of deposit? I remember being so naïve about the economy that I bought my first house at the tender age of 20 and got a 12 ½% mortgage on the property. I didn't understand a whole lot about economics or the fact that things like interest rates were cyclical; I just wanted to own a house. Interest rates are, indeed, cyclical, and just as we should have known that they'd eventually get lower in the 1980s, it is not unreasonable to think that they will eventually go higher from the current historic lows. There are special sets of problems that come along if you own financial assets in a period of rising interest rates, and, while I don't know exactly when rates will go higher, I don't think it takes a genius to say that at some point they will, and you should have some understanding of what that does to assets you may be holding in your retirement accounts.

I remember working at Poster Hardware, in Fairfield Connecticut, while I was in high school and college, in the 1970s. Inflation was running rampant, and Joe Poster, the owner of the store, would complain that he had to pay more to replace some of the things we had just sold off the shelves than he just charged our customers. The President of the United States, Richard Nixon, enacted wage and price controls to combat inflation in 1971, and it backfired. The story of the 1970s economy in the world was one of stagflation: rising inflation and a slowing economy. Although the government tried to enact policies to fix the economy, they achieved almost no success. Throughout the 80s (remember those Whip Inflation Now buttons?) the US economy was in turmoil as the government fought to get runaway inflation and high unemployment under control. Jimmy Carter's appointment of Paul Volcker as chairman of the Federal Reserve Board in 1981 only exacerbated the failing of the economy, and interest rates rose to previously unimagined heights. Today, if you read the official website of the St. Louis Federal Reserve Board, you will see that Paul Volcker is hailed as the hero who saved the economy, but many of us remember the resentment and hatred for the man who caused the prime rate to rise to 21%, unemployment to rise to 12%, and caused our parents so much pain.

We boomers came of age during a period in history when interest rates were recovering from these highs, and we came to accept an environment of high interest rates for mortgages and for certificates of deposit. If you look at the chart at the beginning of this chapter, you'll see, with a few exceptions, interest rates have largely gone down in the shape of the ski slope since the 1980s. An entire generation of money managers and investors have only known what it is like to buy financial assets like stocks and bonds with the backdrop of falling interest rates.

For almost two generations, bond investors have enjoyed a generally benign interest rate environment. As the chart depicts, 20-year T-Bond rates rose from the beginning of the post-WWII era through their peak in 1980 and have been pretty much coming down ever since. The possibility, therefore, arises that contemporary bond investors do not have sufficient experience with rising interest rate environments to properly gauge bond investment risk.

Returns by Decade

The post-war era in the U.S. was one of unbridled economic expansion. Interest rates underwent sustained expansion, especially as the inflation rate began to go higher. Chart 1 indicates that 20-year T-Bond rates actually caught up with, and even overshot, inflation during the go-go 1970's. The turning point was the aforementioned ferocious bear market of 1981, when the stock market and interest rates collapsed. Of course, falling interest rates are great for bond investors. As the following figure shows, the 10-year T-Bond market had relatively low average annual returns during the period of 1951-1980. Going forward, the bond market experienced historically high average annual returns, especially in the period 1981-1990.

Average Annual Returns of 10-Year T-Bonds, by Decade

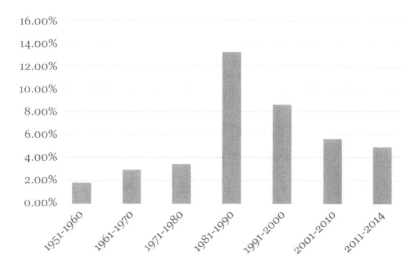

10-YEAR T-BOND RETURNS BY DECADE

While 2009 and 2013 were bad years for bonds, the 2014 return on the 10-year T-Bond was 10.75 percent, a handsome return compared to the 13.48 percent returned by the S&P 500, a mere 2.73 percent spread. If your experience in the bond market doesn't predate 1981, you might have become accustomed to relatively high returns. In fact, since 2000, there have been four years (2000, 2001, 2002 and 2008) in which the T-Bonds outperformed the S&P 500 — in 2008, the bond return of 20.10 percent had a whopping 56.65 percentage point spread above stock returns. Moreover, these returns stemmed from bonds that had no default risk! If the picture painted seems too good to be true, well, it probably is.

Rock Bottom

One prime reason why past may not be prologue is the collapse of short-term interest rates. The three-month T-Bill returned 4.64 percent in 2007, but in 2014 it returned a mere

0.05 percent, well below the inflation rate. With the end of aggressive moves by the Federal Reserve to lower interest rates (known as "quantitative easing") and the (somewhat modest) pickup in the American economy, it looks like bond yields have no place to go but up. Of course, rising interest rates, within limits, help stocks and hurt bonds. A secular change in the bond market may be upon us in which bond prices fall as yields rise to keep up with inflation.

How Rising Interest Rates Hurt Bond Prices

Let me give you a very simple example of why interest rates hurt your investments when they are on the rise: let's say that you bought a bond from your financial guy for $1000. It comes due in 10 years at which time it will pay you back your $1000. While you hold the bond it will pay 5% interest, and there is virtually no risk to principal, as your bond has been issued by a company with a AAA rating. Everything is fine if you hold your bond until it matures. But suppose that while you are holding the bond, interest rates go inexplicably higher, and a new bond, with the same credit rating, that comes due on the same day as yours, is now paying 10% interest. Wouldn't you rather own a bond paying 10% instead of one paying 5%? Of course you would, and so would anyone else. If you wanted to sell your bond so that you could get one of the new higher-paying bonds you would find that, since all other things are equal, no buyers are willing to pay as much for your 5% bond as they would for the 10% bond. Common sense, right? The market value of bonds will go up or down inversely to interest rates. Locking in, for the long term, at today's historically low interest rates will be seen as a particularly horrible investment decision if interest rates eventually go much higher. Of course; this is an extremely simplistic example that I created to make a point, but it's an important concept to grasp as you invest your own money: rising interest rates hurt bond prices.

Most bonds pay a fixed interest rate, called the coupon rate. If interest rates rise after a bond is issued, that bond's fixed coupon starts looking puny, making the bond less desirable. Buyers will demand lower prices to compensate for the bonds relatively low yield. As you no doubt recall, the current yield on a bond is the annual interest payments divided by the market price. As the required yield rises, bond prices must retreat—it's an inverse relationship.

Interest rates reflect the demand for (and supply of) money. As economic activity picks up, so does demand for money to finance business growth and investment. The government doesn't usually print more money, for fear of devaluing the dollar and creating inflation (although that is exactly what they did to respond to the economic crisis of 2008; they called it "quantitative easing"). With a relatively fixed money supply and increasing interest rates, bond buyers will not want to tie up their money in long-term bonds without suitable compensation to cushion them from lower bond prices. The cycle thus reinforces itself: increased economic activity creates more demand for money, higher interest rates, and lower prices on existing bonds. New bonds are issued with higher coupons, creating more interest income for bondholders, which in turn stimulates the economy further.

Unfortunately, a tree doesn't grow to the sky, and interest rates don't increase without limit. At some point, the cost of borrowing exceeds the return on investing the borrowed money, and the economy begins to cool.

During the growth phase, the general level of prices, or inflation, increases as competition for workers and other capital climbs. If you hold bonds that return a rate less than the inflation rate, you are losing money in real terms. No one will buy your bonds unless you drop the price low enough to offer a positive real yield — that is, a yield above the inflation rate. If inflation seems to be getting out of control, the Federal Reserve steps in and decreases the money supply and/or increases the interest rate it charges to banks, either of which is akin to hitting the brakes on the economy. As the risk of an economic slowdown increases, bonds begin to recover in anticipation of interest rates eventually backing down because of decreased demand for money. This might be a good time to buy bonds, but we are certainly not in this situation in early 2015!

The World Is a Risky Place

Rising interest rates also have secondary effects that increase the risk of bond investing:

1. Default Risk: In the current climate of low short-term interest rates, it's not surprising that many bond investors look for ways to increase their interest income. The two obvious ways — buying longer-term bonds and buying lower-quality bonds — both introduce risks to accompany their higher returns. While there is no default risk in switching from T-Bills to T-Bonds, things change when you leave the safe shores of Treasury Debt and set sail into the sea of corporate bonds. Triple-A rated bonds yield a little more than T-Bonds of the same maturity and are still relatively low-risk, though by no means guaranteed. As inflation heats up, the competition for money drives lower-quality companies to issue "junk" high-yield bonds, often with double-digit coupons, and it has horrified me to see retired investors herded into junk bonds by the major marketing organizations of Wall Street. For a segment of bond investors, these bonds seem too good to pass up. But remember; the reason you collect a high coupon on junk bonds is because of the substantial risk that the issuer will default on interest or principle payments, handing you a potentially catastrophic loss. The trade-offs between risk and return in the junk bond market are widely

debated, with some pointing to overall positive returns even with some bonds in a portfolio defaulting. Others see folks with non-diversified portfolios of junk bonds being wiped out. Whatever the outcome, no one can deny that junk bond investing is risky.

2. Competition From Stocks: An economy undergoing orderly growth tends to foster a bullish stock market. Companies are able to raise capital affordably and convert it into profitable income streams, raising the demand for the stock and increasing the likelihood of new or higher dividend payouts. A strong stock market draws money out of bonds as investors look for the best return potential. Of course, many stocks are even riskier than junk bonds — at least the bonds take precedence over stocks if the company is liquidated. To compete, new bonds must have ever-fatter coupons and existing bonds must sell at a greater discount. You might be one of the very rare investors who can time market exit and entry perfectly, switching between stocks and bonds just before the rest of the investing world follows suit. (If you are, give us a phone call!) More likely, you and most other investors will be late to the party and late to leave it, not the type of investing we recommend for most retirees.

3. Reinvestment Risk: If you decide to take the plunge and buy long-term, higher-yielding bonds, even though interest rates are rising, you can reinvest you interest payments at higher rates and thus earn a higher yield to maturity. That works well until it no longer does—a weakening of the economy will eventually depress interest rates, meaning you won't be able to reinvest coupon payments at the same rates as that of the bond. True, the bond price itself should rise, but many investors hold their bonds until maturity, meaning that the damage to their income stream from lower interest rates is permanent. An alternative is zero-coupon bonds, which have no reinvestment risk because they pay no interest until

maturity. However, unless you hold your zeroes in a tax-deferred account like an IRA, you'll have to pay tax each year on the imputed, or "phantom," interest on the bonds. Buying zero coupon bonds in the current interest rate environment is not preferred.

4. Other Risks: If you diversify your bond holdings internationally — usually a good idea — be aware that the issuing country might have a weak currency that reduces the value of your interest payments when you convert them to dollars. If you don't own a diversified portfolio of bonds, then you face heighted risk of being hurt if your particular bonds default. There is also the opportunity risk in holding bonds during a period in which the invested money would have produced a larger return if allocated to different assets.

Reaching for Yield

As I said, many investors have attempted to keep their cash flow high by buying bonds that have extremely low credit ratings, called junk bonds; these bonds will be the first ones to suffer when interest rates go higher because they already carry a larger chance of default. Retirees have been part of this "search for yield" that has led them into credit areas that should frighten any conservative investor. Trying to increase current cash flow by placing principal at risk is an especially bad policy when you consider that any blip up in interest rates will decimate the value of a junk bond portfolio.

A bond trader will tell you that you only have a couple of ways to increase your cash flow when investing in bonds. You can increase your duration (the length of time before your bonds are paid off by the issuer), or you can lower your credit quality. It seems unreasonable, to me, to risk retirement funds by tying up money for longer periods of time or buying bonds that may never return my original investment. Yet, that's what a number of financial salespeople and institutions are recommending right now. I believe that by segmenting retirement into five-year Bins that you can avoid the temptation to buy lower credit quality bonds or to tie your money up for a ridiculous period of time.

Stocks, Rising Interest Rates, and the Battle of Inflation

Let's think for a minute about the environment in which interest rates are rising. There is probably some success in the economy, and rates are going up because of the fear of inflation and, in our particular time in history, because the Federal Reserve Board has stopped propping up the economy after the 2008 financial crisis. Initially, these rising interest rates may manifest themselves in higher stock prices because of the improvement in the economy. But because conservative investors will have an alternative to stock prices, significant amounts of capital may eventually crowd the exits of the stock market and head for safer harbors. Such is the nature of economic cycles and we will start the investment cycle all over again.

I have been arguing, throughout this book, that flexibility is one of the most important attributes your portfolio can possess, and I urge you to be in a position to move some of your assets to safer and higher interest paying financial instruments when and if that time comes. The stock market did not perform well during the 70s and 80s and it wasn't until inflation was under control that the great bull market of our lifetime was born. It can be argued that we are a long way from runaway inflation right now; in fact you could probably argue that we are still in deflationary times, but that doesn't mean that interest rates will stay at historic lows forever. It seems pretty reasonable to think that when a number, no matter what it measures, gets close to zero the next likely move is higher, and it is not unreasonable to suggest that today's low interest rates are paving the road to tomorrow's inflation.

Here's what I watch: wages. If unemployment drops and wages begin to rise, I will begin to have serious concerns about inflation. An old Wall Street money manager, the late Jack McCarthy, one of my investment heroes, early in my career told me that inflation isn't an issue of prices rising; they tend to rise and fall based on demand. Rising labor costs, however, are more permanent and tend to be the harbinger of coming inflation. Inflation is, over time, our main opponent in the battle for retirement survival. During a normal economic recovery (as opposed to Stagflation), stocks are often a good alternative to bonds, and I usually recommend some form of equity investments for Bins 2 through 6.

Being Shareholder Instead of a Trader

There is a world of difference between being a stock trader and a stock investor, at least there should be a difference in your mindset and approach. Speculation, as I define it, involves trying to outguess the next investor and trying to beat him at the game of timely buying and selling. That's fine; all investing involves the concept of buying low and, hopefully, selling higher. However; I believe that actual investing involves a long-term view of the underlying business in which you are investing. Stocks are not simply pieces of paper, they represent ownership in an underlying corporation and stockholders benefit from increasing earnings of that corporation and the relative value of those shares. An investor is not so much buying shares as much as he is buying a business, he views himself as an owner. In the short term, stock prices are valued by the emotions and gyrations of the market; in the long term they are decided by the profitability of the business. That's why I recommend that you only purchase stocks in your Bins that have 6 year or longer time horizons.

What about inflation and investing in stocks instead of bonds or cash equivalents? The world famous investor (and my other investment hero), Warren Buffett remarks that from 1964 through 2014, the S&P 500, including dividends, generated a return of more than 11,000%. Over that same period of time, the U.S. dollar lost 87% of its purchasing power, meaning it now costs $1 to buy what in 1965 cost 13¢. According to Buffett, it has been far more profitable to invest in a collection of American businesses for the past 50 years than to simply own cash. According to Warren, in his 2015 Berkshire Hathaway investment letter, it seems likely that the next 50 years will present the same result. Stocks did not do well in the inflationary 1970's, which was something of an anomaly, but over most meaningful periods of time stocks have outperformed inflation. (There are other strategies to examine in highly inflationary times).

I told you in an earlier chapter that the new Wall Street metric-oriented professionals define volatility as risk, and to some extent they are right. It is bad investment policy to try to fund short-term investments in stocks or bonds: that's why I stress using risk free investments in your first Bin. If, however, you have a longer time frame and can make regular investments in your stock portfolio, Buffet explains that volatility is not risk. The key, I believe, is to invest systematically over-time, here in this office, we almost never invest all of our assets at one time. Only by having a longer term time horizon can you turn volatility from something to be avoided into something that is to be embraced. Over-time, stocks should begin to realize their actual value and reflect the value that you, the brilliant long-term investor, perceived.

We've been talking, at some length, about the dilemma that current retirees face, with interest rates at record lows, and the stock market at record highs. Obviously, it would be crazy for me to recommend that you jump into the stock market with both feet after writing a WHOLE BOOK telling you to be really, really careful about that! However, I suggested that if you are lucky (and disciplined enough) to have a Funded Retirement, your main job is to keep pace with inflation and, secondarily, to replace the assets in your current Bin. Then a systematic and long-term strategy of investing in stocks is difficult to ignore. This strategy, a long-lost and much better mannered cousin of stock-trading, is my preferred method of retirement funding.

Stock trading is about guessing, being right almost all of the time, and it requires constant vigilance. Long-term stock ownership, on the other hand, is about buying good issues, taking a long term view, and having annual or semi-annual reviews. It's not that we don't ever decide to sell the stocks we hold in our long term Bins, but we aren't doing so constantly. Sometimes our issues go up in price quickly, and we decide to use our assets to invest in other under-valued issues. Other times our companies disappoint us, and we decide that we don't want to wait around to see if management can overcome new issues that come along.

As I've stressed, flexibility is crucial to the Bins and Gaps method of investing; knowing the difference between a short term market correction and a bear market requires a certain amount of skill, and I hope you will retain the flexibility to change the investment mix in your Bins if there is a significant sea change in the investment waters. One of the things I like best about equity investing is the relative liquidity, I can sell my shares anytime the markets are open, unlike, say, owning investment real estate. By investing systematically, that is, over periods of time, those of us who invest in equities can slowly build positions and avoid the angst that comes with poor market timing.

The fact that Warren Buffet has made a lot of money in stocks doesn't guarantee that you will too, stock investing involves risk. However, using a disciplined and long term approach to investing is the only way I know of to have any chance of having your retirement portfolio keep pace with inflation. Market conditions are always a concern, and just as I wouldn't load up in a portfolio of bonds under current conditions, there may be times I would be more hesitant to dip my toe in the stock market. Retirement planning, at least the way I do it, is about capital preservation and long term investing, not about stock trading and speculation.

10

THE ENDGAME

**Cause I've had the time of my life.
And I owe it all to you.
The Righteous Brothers**

When you conduct comprehensive retirement planning, without a doubt, the most melancholy task is thinking about your estate; no one really likes to be *that* grown up. We all remember friends and family members who weren't lucky enough to make it to retirement age, and the thought of our own demise isn't something that we like to dwell upon. Financial planning, by its nature, requires some serious and even unpleasant contemplation of circumstances that we would rather not think about, and I promise that this chapter will try to remain upbeat and give you some good ideas to make the transfer of your assets to your loved ones as efficient as possible. (And after spending a few days writing this chapter, I promise that I will need a hard bike ride and a beer!)

Estate Planning

There are a lot of questions that come up about whether you will have to pay taxes through your estate after you die. Let's say this: if you have retirement accounts, somebody, someday, will have to pay income taxes. For most of us, that's it, *estate* taxes are for people with fairly large estates. In 2015 the federal estate planning deduction is $5.43 million for an individual and nearly $11 million for a married couple. If your total estate (the value of everything you own including your home and your investments and even your life insurance) exceeds these amounts then you should see an estate planning professional. Your state estate tax, commonly called the death tax, may also apply to you, and of course that varies from state to state. It is beyond the scope of this book to go deeply into advanced estate planning strategies; so let me just tell you that if you have a potential estate tax due upon your death you should know that professionals call this tax "voluntary," and a little bit of money spent at a lawyer in the proper preparations for your estate can usually avoid any estate tax.

One of the most common questions that I hear, as a Certified Financial Planner™, is whether or not you can gift amounts of money to your friends or family members. Quite simply, if you are not likely to pay the estate tax because your assets are not over the $5.43 million amount then you can give any amount of money to pretty much anybody you want without any estate tax implications. This question comes up because a couple of decades ago the federal estate tax exemption was only about $600,000, and many people in our parents' and grandparents' generations were concerned about paying the estate tax; so we used to hear a LOT about gifting $11,000 to family members. Today, with the higher estate exemptions, the number of people who are potentially on the hook to pay estate taxes is much smaller. As a rule of thumb, I would suggest that, if your estate is anywhere near $5 million, even if you're married because one of you will inherit the estate from the other, you see an estate planning professional to discuss matters like gifting and estate taxes. If you are not, then I suggest that your biggest concern in regards to taxation is income taxes.

Retirement Plan Taxation

In general, any tax-deferred retirement account like an IRA, a 403B, and the 401(k) are all designed to give you a tax break when you deposit your money, and then you are taxed when you withdraw the money. (Roth IRAs are an exception, they do not receive a tax break when you deposit your funds and, instead, are allowed to grow tax-free, and there is never an income tax due upon withdrawal. Even upon death, the proceeds of a Roth IRA are not taxed and while you are living there is no required minimum distribution.) Think of the taxation of your retirement accounts as a tollbooth at the exit to a highway: the tax collector gets his money as you withdraw it.

The funds withdrawn from retirement accounts are taxed as regular income and are subject to the same tax brackets that any other regular income are subject to. So when you take an extremely large sum of money out of your retirement accounts you will pay a relatively high tax rate. We will talk about a couple of ways to minimize this tax, but know that you made a deal with the devil when you deferred taxes: you are trading taxation at a later date for the tax break you received while you were working. In theory, you should be in a lower tax bracket when you are retired; but that's not always the case. Baby boomers, who have put the bulk of their money into their 401(k) plans, may find that while their work related deductions disappeared during retirement, their retirement income needs require them to withdraw money from their retirement accounts at a fairly high tax rate. And, upon death, their heirs will need to remember that distributions from inherited retirement accounts are included in their taxable income for the year. Let me tell you about two methods of setting up your IRA that can help to lessen this pain.

In the first place, your spouse is allowed to roll your entire retirement plan balance into an IRA in his or her own name with no tax consequences. This gets a little more complicated if you are over 70 ½ when you pass away and have begun to take your RMD's. (You'll need to see a tax professional or financial planner about this.) In general, a spouse can continue to use your retirement assets however they choose after you have passed away. Don't forget, a surviving spouse is still subject to the rules regarding RMD's and must combine his or her own retirement plan balance with their inherited funds to calculate their RMD. Of course, you must make sure that your spouse has been named as your beneficiary on your retirement account. This might be a good conversation to have, like, NOW!

Sometimes, if you have left your funds in your company's 401(k), as opposed to rolling into an IRA, your spouse will have the option of leaving the money with the company for a short period of time and sometimes indefinitely. Some company plans force the spouse to take a distribution which can be rolled over into an IRA account. While it is often recommended that a spouse should roll his or her money to an IRA, there are exceptions, and I would again talk with a financial planning professional before I made such a decision. For example, rolling your funds into your own IRA subjects you to the same rules as any IRA, and if you are under 59 ½, you may have to pay a penalty to withdraw funds from the account. But if you make withdrawals, as a widow, from your deceased spouse's retirement plan you may not be subject to that penalty. Make sure that you talk with a financial professional who has some knowledge of these types of rules and can give you unbiased advice regarding the handling of your retirement plan balance.

An alternative to a spousal IRA, and our other method of reducing income tax on large IRA distributions, is often called a "Stretch" or "Beneficiary" IRA. This inherited IRA provides a way to take funds from a retirement account without withdrawing a large lump sum all at once. It works like this: the beneficiary of an inherited IRA, if it is a real person and not a trust or estate, is allowed to withdraw funds from an IRA based on their own life expectancy formula. They must take this minimum amount from the account every year (and include it in their taxable income); this amount goes up every year as they get older. The beneficiaries are allowed to take out any amount over this minimum amount, at any time, but they must at least withdraw the minimum amount every year. So Joe's daughter, Mindy, is 45 years old and is the beneficiary on her dad's $500,000 IRA. Mindy is a professional actress and, at least at the moment, does not need the cash in the IRA, because of her high income. She would pay the highest income tax rate possible if she simply cashed in her inherited IRA. Mindy's financial planner told her about the Stretch IRA and tells her that each year she must withdraw a minimum amount based on the account's year end value and her current age. The rest of the money remains in the account and can be managed for her benefit; she just has to remember her annual withdrawals. This is a powerful estate planning tool that you should tell your kids about because it will, ultimately, aid in their decision as to how to withdraw retirement funds. I should tell you that the rules about Stretch IRAs are a little more complicated than I have just described, and again, you need to do some research, or talk to a financial professional before actually jumping in.

The stretch IRA allows generations to benefit from the savings you made during your working years, and making plans to minimize the taxes on the money upon withdrawal is not only prudent, but powerful. The stretch IRA can be set up with several beneficiaries in mind, each of them having their own account and making their own decisions, so even grandchildren can make withdrawals based upon their life expectancy. Having the bulk of your funds continue to grow on a tax-deferred basis is a powerful alternative to making a lump sum withdrawal and paying a significant amount of income tax. If there was ever a good financial topic to hold an uncomfortable family meeting about, this might be it. The power of tax deferral over several generations is significant, and if your family chooses to treat your IRA account balance as a source of lifetime wealth, instead of a short-term windfall, they will see significant benefits.

Probate

If you work with an estate planning attorney, he will be happy to revel you in hours of stories about celebrities who have not properly planned their estate and whose financial affairs have gone through the time consuming and expensive public process of probate. One of the most significant advantages of retirement accounts is that you do get to name a beneficiary. Financial instruments that have a named beneficiary do not have to go to probate; they get paid directly to the named beneficiary. So for one thing, if your current beneficiary on your retirement accounts is "estate," I would suggest that you find a different and, if possible, human beneficiary. Might I also suggest that you go back and check all of your insurance policies, retirement accounts, and corporate pension accounts that may be in your name to make sure that the people who you currently want to leave your money to are your current beneficiaries. The insurance policy your parents bought for you when you were a kid might still have your parents listed as the beneficiary.

If you have assets, like stocks or bonds, in a brokerage account that are not part of your retirement plan (that is: they are not in an IRA or other tax qualified account), then I would suggest you look into a "TOD" account. A Transfer on Death Account gives you the opportunity to name a beneficiary upon your death, again avoiding probate, while still giving you the option of controlling your assets while you are alive. This is a simple and low cost method streamlining the disposition of your assets upon your death because, again, TOD accounts are not subject to the probate process.

Life Insurance

The proceeds of a life insurance policy are not subject to income tax unless you hold that insurance policy in a tax-deferred account. While buying life insurance in a retirement plan is not a common practice, if you have done so you should know that the proceeds of this type of policy are taxed as income upon withdrawal from the account, just like any other retirement plan proceeds. With that exception in mind, it's nice to know that almost any other insurance policy's death benefit will not be subject to income tax when paid out. Life insurance is considered part of your estate, and if your death benefit will push the value of your estate over that $5.43 million level you should make sure that you do the proper estate planning to avoid taxation on this amount.

The Loss of a Spouse

Sorry to have to talk about another melancholy subject, but, unless you and your spouse are one of those lucky couples that dies together, there are going to be financial consequences when one of you passes away. While the loss of a spouse may mean that some of your living expenses go down, there are probably corresponding losses in income. For one thing, one of your Social Security checks is going to disappear. A surviving spouse does have the option of choosing to continue to collect her own check or, if her spouse's check was higher, choosing his; either way, one of the checks goes away. Sometimes a spouse also loses out on collecting any more of the deceased spouse's pension if no provisions were made for her when he elected his pension options. (We especially see this when couples marry after these retirement options were selected.) The loss of these checks can be especially painful if your retirement was Unfunded and may force the surviving spouse into making decisions like selling a home or other assets.

A good retirement plan should take the possibility of the loss of one spouse into account. The reason we talk about "growth of income" when designing a retirement plan is for contingencies like this. Even if your personal cost of living is relatively stable and not subject to the inflation rate the government publishes every year, the loss of a spouse and their income will surely provide the need for increased income from financial assets. Your retirement plan budget and your Lifetime Gap should be recalculated at this point and adjustments made to the income withdrawn from your retirement account or from other assets. In my own planning practice, I have found that fixed, guaranteed annuities provide a good vehicle for deferring income until an event like this. Life insurance, growth investments, and other financial vehicles can also be earmarked for this contingency.

Pension Maximization

If you do have the opportunity to collect a lifetime income from a pension you are, indeed, lucky! Usually at the time that you decide to collect your pension you are given a series of choices regarding the size of your monthly check. The highest monthly payment will be attached to something called the "Single Life Option." This means that when the person drawing the pension check dies, the checks stop coming. The other options are various choices based upon what happens when you die. For a smaller monthly check the pensioner has the option of having his surviving spouse continue to collect a monthly check. This is a really good option, but not always the best one to choose. Basically, the insurance company providing your lifetime income is buying an insurance policy on your life, and that's why the monthly check for this option is considerably smaller.

Pension maximization is a strategy used by financial planners to provide income for your spouse after your death, while getting the highest pension payment for yourself. The concept is that if we can find a way to buy enough insurance to replace your maximum option, single life, then should you die first your spouse will receive an uninterrupted income stream from an insurance policy. And if your spouse should predecease you, you will have the option of cashing in that insurance policy and continue to receive your monthly pension income. The numbers don't always work out, and you have to make sure that you have the discipline to continue to pay a new insurance policy throughout retirement, but a pension maximization strategy might work for you. Here's an example:

John will have the option of collecting $1600 a month in his single life pension option. His joint life option, with his wife, is $1200 a month. If he can buy a large enough insurance policy to replace $1200 a month for the rest of his wife's life for less than the difference in his two options ($400), he may decide to collect the larger amount and initialize the pension maximization strategy. Should he pass away before his wife she will earn the same income as they were from the investment of the life insurance proceeds. If she should predecease John he will have the option of cashing in his policy or naming one of his children as new beneficiary and continuing the policy by making further premium payments. He will continue to collect the $1600 a month pension income.

Pension maximization is an especially favorite tool of insurance sales professionals, and I would carefully examine all of my options before buying a policy and especially before selecting an option on my pension. If you choose the single life option and then can't get a corresponding life insurance policy because of health reasons, you will have a bitter spouse on your hands for the rest of your retirement. A professional who does not have a stake in the game through the insurance sale, like a Certified Financial Planner™, a CPA, or an estate planning attorney are good independent people to help you make this decision. Also; you must have the proper discipline to pay the premiums on the new insurance policy for the rest of your retirement.

His, Hers, and Ours

Good financial planning, with regards to the disposition of your assets at death, can prevent family feuds, hard feelings, and other avoidable potential disasters. Since comparatively few people make it all the way through retirement having been married to the same person for their entire life, the need for some simple estate planning at retirement age is crucial. Whether I work with couples who remarried before retirement or after, it is important that blended families make provisions when it comes to the disposition of retirement assets.

There's a term in financial planning called "Estate Equalization," and it is a powerful thing to know about. Let's say that our new friend John is predeceased by his wife and remarries a wonderful woman he meets in his retirement community. John has just one daughter, but his new wife, also a widow, raised four kids. John's daughter, Meg, is concerned that her new stepmom might inherit all of his, and her mom's, retirement accounts, as well as their other assets. If all of the assets are simply left to all 5 of the new couple's children, Meg does not feel that it is fair to split her assets five ways since she was an only child. She wishes her dad well and is happy that he has found someone in his life, but she has legitimate concerns about what happens to the family money after her dad dies. John, on the other hand, is very concerned about taking care of his new wife and wants to make sure that he leaves her financially healthy. Potentially, there is a problem here that could create a family riff that lasts forever. Let's see if some financial planning can solve this problem.

The first thing that a financial planner should do when looking at John and his new wife's financial situation is recalculate their ability to fill their financial obligations and figure out if it is possible to classify their retirement as "Funded" or "Unfunded". If we assume that John and his new wife (let's call her Margaret) are combining two households and able to cut down on expenses, we would probably be safe to say that they have a Funded Retirement. If their current expenditures are covered by Social Security and pension payments the planner should next take into consideration required minimum distributions from each of their IRAs and what would happen to the household if one of the parties were to pass away. In other words, he would employ the Bins and Gaps method of retirement planning.

After consulting a tax attorney and an estate attorney, our financial planner might decide that the best way to take care of this married couple (and the concerns of John's daughter) would be through life insurance contracts on John and his new bride. Life insurance has evolved in the last several decades and a new class of senior life insurance is available that is designed to provide a death benefit at a much more reasonable cost than you might have thought. In this case, the planner will use John's and Margaret's Required Minimum Distributions (from their IRA accounts) each year to fund a life insurance policy for the projected value of each of their retirement accounts. In the event of one of their deaths, the life insurance policy would pay their children a lump sum that is income tax free. The surviving spouse would take advantage of the spousal IRA and inherit the other's retirement account and use it to continue to fund their living expenses. The surviving spouse will have the option to continue his/her own life insurance policy, and name his/her own children as beneficiaries, or cash in and stop making premium payments. The survivor will also be allowed to name whomever they choose as the beneficiary of their retirement account.

It would be wonderful if all estate planning situations could be solved so easily as my hypothetical case above, but it has been my experience that with a little planning, estate equalization is worth the cost of any insurance or legal documents.

Sometimes we run into married couples who are concerned about leaving equal amounts of money to their own children and they don't feel that simply naming beneficiaries to their retirement accounts is a reasonable solution. For example, if a husband and wife built a family business together and left that business to their child who manages it; the remaining child might feel that they have been slighted because they did not go into the family business. In this case; a type of insurance policy called "second to die life" is used to pay that child an amount equal to the value of the business—a life insurance policy that only pays its benefit when both parents pass away. Second to die life insurance is a relatively low cost life insurance planning tool that is often easier to underwrite than a single life insurance policy because it is ensuring two lives. Couples who have a significant surplus in their retirement savings, say in a collection of tax-deferred annuities, often fund this type of life insurance with these dollars. When used effectively, life insurance can increase the size of an estate and provide funds for things like grandchildren's education and charitable endeavors.

Often, it is necessary to involve an estate attorney or trust company to take care of contingencies that might arise in a slightly more complicated family situation. There are times that parents want to protect their children from themselves and utilize a trust to pay out their retirement assets periodically or to protect them in case of a divorce or other complications. You can design a trust that is attached to an IRA, and I am hesitant to give you any more advice about the subject without referring you to an estate planning professional. There is a limit as to how much wisdom I can impart to you in a book like this, and I'm afraid that you will need specific guidance situation that can only be given by an expert in the field. The important thing is that you know that there is the possibility that you have some control over where your money goes after your death.

I'm Going to Live Forever – Fame

Before we go rushing you off to the funeral parlor let's discuss the very real chance that you might live a lot longer than you planned. The fastest growing demographic, by percentage, in the world is centenarians, and with all of the medical advances in modern science it is not inconceivable that you might comfortably live past 100 years old. Estate planning is only useful if you have enough assets to distribute at the end of your life, and one of the things that is crucial to any retirement plan is that you don't outlive your principal. I've spent enough time in this chapter talking about life insurance, which is the insurance that you buy to cover your family's losses should you die too soon, and it is reasonable now to talk about annuities, which is insurance against outliving your money.

Through the Bins and Gaps Retirement Planning Method, it is possible to plan to replace the income spent from your current Bin through the investment performance of your longer-term Bins. At a bare minimum, we have designed our retirement plan so that it has enough capital to last until your 100th birthday. After your 100th birthday, your retirement plan is only as good as your investment performance, your retirement budget, and your burn rate. One way to protect yourself from outliving your capital is to purchase a deferred or immediate annuity from an insurance company. Annuity contracts can be bought as joint life policies or based on a single life, and some can have built-in cost-of-living adjustments. Of course, your monthly checks are based upon your current age (and current interest rates) and are becoming more popular as people live longer and investment returns become harder to chase. I only mention them here, in this section on retirement planning, because there are a few issues that come up when a person inherits an annuity.

An annuity lives in two phases, sort of like a butterfly. During the accumulation phase, the annuity, like a caterpillar building a chrysalis, builds up capital to eventually provide a lifetime income. During the income phase the annuitant receives an income based upon his/her life expectancy. Once an annuity is annuitized, the annuitant has traded the accumulated value of the annuity for a lifetime income. For that reason, a relatively small percentage of deferred annuities are ever annuitized. Rather, a client will make a series of withdrawals and hope that the performance of their annuity each year makes up for the amount withdrawn. Some newer contracts provide a rider that pays a guaranteed income for life in the amount being withdrawn, based upon the owner's age. The estate planning questions come into play when someone dies while owning an annuity that is in the accumulation phase.

Annuities come in two flavors: qualified and nonqualified. A qualified annuity is part of a retirement plan, for example, it may have been purchased inside of an IRA. And a nonqualified annuity was purchased with dollars that were not already part of a tax-deferred vehicle. Whether qualified or nonqualified, individual insurance contract in the individual insurance company who wrote the contract will stipulate how soon the dollars in the contract must be withdrawn. Like other insurance products, annuities do have named beneficiaries and will often give them the ability to withdraw funds over a series of years or even life expectancy. Some contracts require annuitization, even by the beneficiary, to avoid significant withdrawal charges.

I have often been concerned that people with no current income tax issues during retirement are being sold so many annuities, thanks to those ubiquitous free luncheon seminars for seniors. I worry that they may have tax-deferred their way into income tax issues at estate settlement time. Annuities are relatively complicated contracts, and when used properly they are powerful retirement planning tools. If you ever inherit one, be very careful about the taxation and withdrawal charges that come between you and the money you are about to receive. While a spouse can move money from an annuity in a qualified IRA to her own IRA after the death of her spouse, she may still be charged withdrawal fees for doing so. Withdrawing money from a nonqualified IRA, which usually doesn't have spousal provision, involves taking out taxed principle and tax-deferred earnings. A simple withdrawal of funds pays taxable interest first and principle last. If the contract is "annuitized," (over, say five years) principal and interest are paid out together, a possible tax advantage.

The safety and tax deferral of annuities are often offset by high surrender fees and the long-term nature of these contracts. Like just about everything in the world (except love), you can get too much of a good thing and there are only so many annuities necessary in a retiree's portfolio. A number of government regulators are concerned that annuities are being oversold to older investors, and I hope that you will make sure that you are not over-invested in this particular area. And furthermore, if you own annuities it is important that you properly name your beneficiaries and include them in any estate planning that you find necessary.

Please forgive my rant, let's get back to the reason I brought it up, which is living forever. If you buy an annuity that begins paying you checks next month; you are immediately getting your own money back. Obviously, an insurance company is not going to pay you a high rate of interest on funds that they have to begin paying back to you right away. The formula that calculates the size of your lifetime check is based on current interest rates, and of course, right now, those rates are very low. The real value of an immediate annuity is that it pays you no matter how long you live. That's why I have suggested that you wait a while before purchasing an immediate annuity, and perhaps when you get to your second or third Bin your advanced age (and possible higher interest rates) will make annuities more attractive than they are right now.

Keep in mind that your risk in purchasing an immediate annuity is that you may forfeit the principle that might other-wise be left to your heirs. If you purchase a lifetime annuity at age 65 and have the unfortunate circumstances to die a year later, your heirs will derive no benefit from that annuity. (Yes it's a little more complicated than that, you can pick things like "period certain annuities" that have some estate benefits. But in general, your heirs will derive little benefit from funds that you have annuitized.) Like I said a few times in this book, risk is not a bad word; you just have to understand the risks and trade-offs you get with anything you invest your money in. In my world, right now annuities are not as attractive as they have been at other times in my career.

I'm Glad We Had This Chat

Estate planning is awfully hard to dress up as something to get excited about. I don't enjoy talking to my clients about their impending deaths nor do I like thinking about my own. Sometimes, as I warned my children, being a grown-up sucks. The powerful thing about doing a little bit of estate planning is that you can leave a positive lasting impression on your children and grandchildren. If you aren't blessed with family, or don't want to leave them any money, a little planning can ensure that the people who you want to see inherit your funds get them. After 30 years in the financial services industry, I have yet to meet a beneficiary who turns down a check, but I have noticed that the heirs who receive funds in a prompt manner, with little administrative costs, and a minimum of income taxes, are appreciative of the efforts taken by the person who left them the funds.

Some of the estate planning tools I've mentioned, like stretch IRAs and estate equalization, give you the ability to create true generational wealth and make up for a life of hard work that didn't always allow you to give your children and grandchildren everything that you wished you could. If you are married, the benefits of making sure that your spouse has as little financial hardship as possible after you are gone is a reward in and of itself. I suspect that if you have stayed this far with this chapter, that you have already made plans or are considering making plans to take care of the people you love. I'm proud of you, and I hope I've helped.

11

PLEASE PACK YOUR KNIVES AND GO

Tramps like us, baby we were born to run
Bruce

Did you know that self-help books, like this one, are only supposed to be 10 chapters? I can't help it; that's the law. It's a shame that I have to go now; I was feeling like we were just getting to know one another! But it seems that people don't like to read anything longer than 140 characters anymore, and books? Well, nobody but us old people buy books anymore. At the risk of staying too long at the party, I have a few more things to tell you—things that are important to talk about, but things that don't really deserve chapters of their own. I wrote *The Retirement Dilemma* to answer a very real question: can I retire right now, and if I do, what am I supposed to do with my money? I'd like to think that I've given you, with the Bins and Gaps Method, a simple, back of the envelope way to answer that question, and, in the time we have left together, I'd like to answer a few more of the questions that I hear often from the people I talk to.

Early Retirement

I know a lady who has been in the same job for over 30 years, and even though she is only 55 years old, she told me she was going to retire and wanted to know what I thought. Well, it turns out, she didn't really want to know what I thought, because when I began to give her an overview of the Bins and Gaps method she just rolled her eyes and changed the subject. I found out later that she really didn't have any retirement savings at all and simply planned to get a part time job to supplement her pension income until she could collect Social Security at 62; in other words, she was not going to do *even one thing* that I recommend in this book. Not one. Sigh... prophets really aren't listened to in their home towns.

The other shock to my system was the event of an old high school friend's Mother's passing, and when I placed my condolence on his Facebook page I saw a lot of people, who I hadn't thought of since high school, who were also passing along their sympathies. After a few minutes of cyber-stalking; I was absolutely amazed at how many of them were also retired, well before 60 years old, and I began to feel pretty lucky to have a career that is still stimulating and still pays the bills. I can't imagine retiring for a long, long time. But that's me, and I understand that not everyone has a choice about their retirement date, and some of us have jobs that we just can't wait to leave. That being said, there are still some crucial decisions to make about an early retirement—decisions that will affect your cash flow for the rest of your life.

So what do we mean by early retirement? Some of my classmates didn't seem to be retired as much as they were simply downsized and gave up on looking for another job; others had put in military careers and had nice pensions, and still others were simply looking for a change in life and wanted to try something new, even if it didn't pay much. Since I am a financial planning type of guy, and this is a financial planning book, let's talk a little bit about those early retirement decisions.

First off, unless you are legally disabled, there is a 10% penalty if you begin to withdraw from your Individual Retirement Accounts before you reach age 59 ½. That penalty is taxed as income, so you pay tax on the penalty too, and when you add income tax and state income tax onto the amount of money you withdraw from your plan, it gets very expensive to retire early. There is an exception; it's called "Rule 72T," a provision in the tax code that allows for early withdrawal from your IRA, provided you schedule your withdrawals as "substantially equal payments" over at least a 5 year period, and they must continue, at least until you reach age 59 ½. These withdrawals must still be based on life expectancy, in other words you may only withdraw an amount based on the IRS life expectancy tables, a relatively low number if you are only in your fifties. And if your withdrawals end before the end of the five year period, or before you turn 59 ½, you will have to go back to the very first dollar you withdrew and charge yourself the 10% penalty. All of the distributions, of course, are taxable as income, whether you are penalized or not. Here's a link to the IRS webpage to explain more.

If you have been reading along with me so far, you'll know that the significant factor in all of this, at least to me, is the provision that if you take funds out of your retirement plan before 59 ½, you will have to take the income based on life expectancy. Quite simply, you are expected to live longer at age 55 than at age 65, and you end up cutting the same retirement account pie into smaller pieces when you begin to collect at a younger age. The same thing happens with Social Security, if you begin to collect at 62 you will get smaller payments for the rest of your life than you will at age 70. If you decide to retire early you may also be deciding to receive smaller pension payments for the rest of your life. Traditional pension plans are not only based on your years of service but on your life expectancy, so again, you will receive a smaller check if you begin to collect when you are younger.

Health Care Costs

Here's the other cost associated with retiring early: Medicare doesn't kick in until you are 65 years old. If your former employer doesn't pay for your health insurance after retirement (an increasingly rare benefit), you'll have to pay it. Although you can't be denied coverage due to a pre-existing condition, thanks to the Affordable Care Act, your cost will be relatively high: CNN estimates that a couple who retires at age 62, instead of 65, will face an extra $51,000 in insurance costs. In fact, even if you wait until 65 to retire, Fidelity Investments estimates that a couple, in good health, who lives to be 82, and 85 years old, respectively, will spend an average of $220,000 in healthcare costs during retirement. Those with chronic health issues, or those who live longer, can expect to spend more. (http://money.cnn.com/2014/06/12/retirement/retirement-health-care/).

Medicare, it should be noted, is part of the Social Security System, as opposed to Medicaid, which is a backstop for poor people; you have to spend down your assets to almost nothing if you want to use it. According to the site http://www.medicare.gov, it is mostly available to people age 65 or older. Part A (Hospital Insurance) covers hospital stays, care in a skilled nursing facility, hospice care, and some home health care. Part B (Medical Insurance) covers certain doctors' services, outpatient care, medical supplies, and preventive services. Part C is a type of Medicare health plan offered by a private company that contracts with Medicare to provide you with all your Part A and Part B benefits. Medicare Advantage Plans include Health Maintenance Organizations, Preferred Provider Organizations, Private Fee-for-Service Plans, Special Needs Plans, and Medicare Medical Savings Account Plans. If you're enrolled in a Medicare Advantage Plan, Medicare services are covered through the plan and aren't paid for under Original Medicare. Most Medicare Advantage Plans offer prescription drug coverage. Part D adds prescription drug coverage to Original Medicare, some Medicare Cost Plans, some Medicare Private-Fee-for-Service Plans, and Medicare Medical Savings Account Plans. These plans are offered by insurance companies and other private companies approved by Medicare. Medicare Advantage Plans may also offer prescription drug coverage that follows the same rules as Medicare Prescription Drug Plans.

Most people get premium-free Part A; in other words, you probably don't incur an extra cost if you are already collecting Social Security. You can get premium-free Part A at 65 if:

• You already get retirement benefits from Social Security or the Railroad Retirement Board.

• You're eligible to get Social Security or Railroad benefits but haven't filed for them yet.

• You or your spouse had Medicare-covered government employment.

Most people get Part B for $104.90 per month, with a $147 a year deductible. If you don't sign up for Part B when you're first eligible, you may have to pay a late enrollment penalty. If your modified adjusted gross income as reported on your IRS tax return from 2 years ago (the most recent tax return information provided to Social Security by the IRS) is above a certain amount, you may pay more. You will need to shop around to get prices on Part B and C coverage.

It's Your Call

So, again, this book is a judgment free zone: you can retire whenever you want as far as I am concerned, but know that the amount of income you collect during retirement will probably be significantly less during retirement than if you wait a while longer to collect. Some people might do better to get a full-time job in a different field after retirement and wait to collect their traditional pension income until a later age, others might find that they can wait to collect Social Security until they reach full retirement age, even though they are collecting their traditional pension. I hope you get out a calculator and do a little math before you make these important decisions!

Preparing For Retirement

Before you retire, at any age, I hope you have taken the time to do a practice retirement and to construct an Anticipated Retirement Budget; those are givens. But, what else can you do? Here's a bullet list of some things to look into in the years leading up to retirement:

1. Pay down any debt that you have, especially consumer debt.

1. If you have a mortgage, look at your re-financing options, just in case there are better options available to you.

2. Max out your pension contributions, look at catch up provisions, and look into Roth IRA accounts.

3. Find your passion: what will make you jump out of bed every day in retirement?

4. Get a physical.

5. Vacation in the places that you are considering retiring to.

6. Check your beneficiaries.

7. Have a full, holistic financial review incorporating retirement planning, tax planning, insurance reviews, and estate planning.

8. Meet with H.R. and make sure you know all of your retirement options.

9. Set some goals: fitness, intellectual, travel, etc. Don't become a couch potato!

Financial Planning for Recent Widows

On average, wives outlive their husbands by four to five years, so it's most likely a surviving spouse is a widow rather than a widower. For whatever the reasons, it seems like many widows were never involved with the family's financial planning. That means a widow must first get over the shock of her husband's death and then face the helpless feeling of assuming control of her finances without sufficient knowledge. Obviously, we encourage all married couples to jointly plan their finances, retirements and arrangements for surviving the death of the spouse.

Picking up the Pieces

OK, you know that you and your husband should have worked together to establish your financial plans, but what if you didn't? We'll look at a few decisions you need to make, but our strongest advice is to immediately engage the services of a trusted financial planner to help you sort out your financial resources and obligations. Together, you and your planner can work out your current assets, employer benefits, annuities and insurance from your deceased husband, your options regarding income and investments, tax considerations and your own estate plan. That's a pretty big nut to crack, but a Certified Financial Planner (CFP) has the expertise and experience to restore financial order during a time of crisis.

Retirement Accounts

Let's start with individual retirement accounts and assume you are the sole beneficiary of your husband's traditional IRA. The easiest course of action is to roll the inherited IRA into your own. If you don't have an IRA, you can simply take title to your husband's account. The benefit is that you don't have to withdraw money from the IRA until you reach age 70 1/2, at which point you must take required minimum distributions (RMDs) based upon your life expectancy. There is no tax impact from an inherited traditional IRA until the money is distributed. If your husband left you assets from an employer plan, such as a 401(k), 403(b) or 457, you can have the plan's trustee transfer the plan's assets to your IRA tax-free.

The rules are different if you inherit a Roth IRA. The income tax has already been paid on the money in the Roth IRA, so generally you face no tax bill. However, any unqualified Roth distributions are subject to taxes—these arise for Roth accounts that are less than five years old. You can't roll an inherited Roth IRA into a traditional IRA, only into a Roth IRA. Even though a Roth IRA owner is not subject to RMDs, as the beneficiary, you are. Some employer plans use Roth accounts and these can be rolled into a Roth IRA.

The 10 percent early withdrawal penalties are automatically waived on all inherited IRAs. If you husband failed to name anyone as the account beneficiary, it will revert to you, the spouse. In certain states, a spouse can't name someone other than you as the beneficiary of an IRA unless you agree to it, in writing. Qualified employer plans always revert to the spouse unless she waives the right.

One interesting twist on inherited IRAs has to do with disclaiming them. For example, suppose you and your second husband each have children, but neither of you adopted the other's children. Your husband names you as the IRA beneficiary and his own children as contingent beneficiaries — they would receive the money if you died before the IRA was distributed. However, you can disclaim the IRA within nine months of your husband's death, and, if it was set up under certain rules known as per stirpes, it reverts to your heirs, presumably your children, rather than to the children of your late second husband. You can also choose to partially disclaim an inheritance. This kind of situation could end up in probate court, and the ruling might not follow the dictates of a will your late second husband might have left behind.

Annuities

An annuity pays income for a fixed period, for the lifetime of the owner, or, in the case of a joint annuity, it continues payments for the lifetime of the beneficiary. The beneficiary payments may be the same or different from those your husband was receiving. Often, the annuity provider allows the surviving spouse to take the cash value of the annuity as a lump-sum payment. The taxes on payments, whether lump sum or annuitized, depend on how much of your husband's contributions to the annuity were already taxed. Contributions to a retirement plan annuity are usually tax-deductible, so distributions would be fully taxable. If your husband instead purchased a joint annuity directly from an insurance company, you will owe taxes on only part of the money you receive — your financial planner or tax accountant will help you work out the calculations.

Most annuities, with or without survivor benefits, provide a death benefit, which may or may not be taxable, depending upon the way the annuity was set up. For example, the proceeds from a non-refundable annuity contract with a face value equal to the single premium are taxable. You can take the death benefit as a lump sum or spread it out through monthly payments.

Life Insurance

You generally do not have to pay income taxes on money left to you by your husband's life insurance policy. This is also true for death benefits paid by worker's comp, endowments, employer group plans, and accident insurance contracts. However, if the insurance premiums were paid with pre-tax money—say, in an employer retirement account—the portion of the payout that represents the cash value of the policy might be taxable. If your husband is the owner of the insurance policy, the proceeds will be included in his estate. You won't be hit with an estate tax because of the spousal exclusion, but your beneficiaries might be. The easiest way to avoid having the life insurance proceeds included in your husband's estate is to ensure that he makes you the owner of the policy at least three years prior to his demise.

Social Security

You may be entitled to Social Security survivor's benefits when you husband dies. You can access these as early as age 60 (or 50 if you are disabled), but the longer you wait, the more they'll build up. If you are entitled to your own retirement benefit, you can take the survivor's benefit while waiting to switch to your own, thereby allowing your own benefit to increase. The amount of the survivor's benefit is reduced if your husband had started taking Social Security benefits before age 66.

You also may be able to receive SSDI widow's benefits if your husband was disabled at the time of death. The rules and amounts are complicated, but your CFP will untangle the mess for you. If your husband was a veteran, you may be eligible for a survivor's pension — check with the Department of Veterans Affairs for more details.

Social security benefits may also be available to divorced widows, depending upon how long you were married before the divorce and whether you ever remarried.

Property

Normally, your husband's property will become yours upon his death. If he makes up a will leaving the property to someone else, you can usually contest it, because the law protects surviving spouses from being disinherited. If you live in a community property state, half of the property owned or purchased during the marriage belongs to you, notwithstanding any other wills, trusts or deeds. Your husband can name a different beneficiary for his half of the community property.

Trustees

It may be that you are not mentally competent to financially handle an inheritance. Your husband may have set up a trust before he died naming a trustee to manage the estate on your behalf. If you disagree with the arrangement, you can go to court and prove your case. Spendthrift trusts are sometimes set up if the husband or divorced husband understands that the wife has a compulsive spending problem, like gambling or drugs. The trust protects the undistributed amount from creditors and doles out only a small income stream to the beneficiary.

What to Do Now

You and your CFP should work together to figure out a monthly budget and how to fund it. Ideally, you would like to maintain your current lifestyle for the remainder of your own life. You may wish for your CFP to structure lump-sum payouts as monthly annuities with inflation protection so that you know you will be receiving a certain amount of real income each month. You can set up various investment and savings accounts to create additional earnings. If you are lucky enough to have or inherit surplus funds, a CFP will help you explore various alternatives, such as trusts, endowments and charitable gifts.

Financial Planning for Non-Traditional Couples

In June of 2013, the Supreme Court ruled in U.S. v Windsor that same-sex couples can be recognized as married in states that have deemed it legal. This opened the door for married same-sex couples (MSSC) to enjoy the benefits and responsibilities of federal recognition of marriage–by some estimates gaining access to more than 1,100 federal protections and benefits. As of this writing, 36 states have legalized same-sex marriage and 14 states ban it.

From the point of view of financial planning, many of the details hinge on whether a non-traditional couple is legally married, although the broad goals are the same: wealth creation, retirement planning, tax strategies, saving for life events, trust and estate planning, family business succession and contingency handling (including breakups, divorces and child custody disputes). Of course, the problems faced by same-sex couples transcend financial planning, as they touch upon many other important matters like visitation rights and heath care/end of life issues, but this article will focus on the financial aspects. Further, let's stipulate that, for the most part, MSSCs currently living in the 39 states that recognize their marriages can perform financially planning just as if they were heterosexual couples, although some exceptions may exist. Thus, we want to zoom in on the unique financial planning challenges faced by unmarried same-sex couples, civil unions and domestic partnerships.

Federal Benefits

Social Security benefits are an important adjunct to most retirement plans. Non-married partners do not receive Social Security spousal benefits, which affects how much each partner can receive while alive and survivor benefits after one partner dies. For example, it's often advantageous when one spouse has a much greater earning history than does the other for the latter to elect spousal benefits based on the former's work record. Non-married couples don't receive this benefit. The same lack of benefits holds if the surviving partner is disabled or is raising the child of the deceased partner.

Same sex unmarried partners don't receive the benefit of the Family and Medical Leave Act, which allows an employee to take time off to attend to an ailing spouse. Of course, nothing prevents a company from granting the leave to an unmarried employee, but it would be a privilege, not a right. Without this benefit, caretaking partners risk losing their jobs and their livelihoods by taking time off to care for an unmarried partner, creating a substantial financial challenge.

Retirement Accounts

Inherited IRAs and employer retirement accounts such as 401(k)s can be folded into a surviving spouse's IRA, thereby postponing required minimum distributions, and the accompanying taxes, until the spouse reaches age 70 1/2. Non-spouse beneficiaries usually have no more than five years before an inherited retirement account must be distributed. Obviously, this creates very different planning scenarios for married vs unmarried couples, whatever their genders. A work-around is possible using properly structured "see-though" trusts. These require expertise to set up correctly and may not have all the benefits of the spousal inheritance. There are also alternatives involving life insurance trusts as a way for one spouse to secure the finances of the surviving spouse. Once again, expertise is required to ensure that these function as desired.

Another benefit of retirement accounts is early withdrawal due to financial hardships. An employee can take an early withdrawal when the medical, funeral, or educational bills of a spouse create a hardship, although a 10 percent penalty is usually assessed if the employee is not yet age 59 1/2. An unmarried employee would likely be unable to access a hardship withdrawal based upon the partner, although it's possible (and often preferable) to arrange a loan from the employer retirement plan.

You can't borrow from an IRA, but you can access the funds at any time, even if you have to pay the 10 percent penalty for early withdrawal. That penalty is waived for withdrawals due to certain medical and educational expenses for you, your spouse or other family members, but not for unmarried partners.

Wealth Transfer

An individual, while alive or upon dying, can transfer an unlimited amount of wealth to a spouse without creating an estate tax or gift tax liability. Annual gifts to an unmarried partner in excess of $14,000 trigger gift tax, but fortunately everyone enjoys a lifetime exemption of $5.43 million (as of 2015) (Ref 3). The same amount is excluded from estate tax.

A married couple can split-gift up to $28,000 per recipient without worrying about which spouse writes the check. Non-married partners don't have this luxury.

A surviving spouse receives the benefit of the deceased partner's unused lifetime exclusion, a benefit known as "portability." An unmarried surviving partner doesn't receive this benefit.

Obviously, these considerations predominantly affect the wealthy, but nonetheless can mean a tax bill for an unmarried partner that would not be assessed if the partner were a spouse. All sorts of trusts are available to work around these problems, and one must assume that if you are wealthy enough to trigger estate and gift taxes, you can afford to pay a competent specialist to structure your trusts for the maximum benefit.

However, sometimes the gift and estate rules affect those who are less than wealthy. For example, suppose a same-sex couple buys a home together and shares equally in the title as joint owners with right to survivorship. In this example, only one of the partners is supplying the funds for the purchase. That partner, let's call her Pat, is considered to have gifted 50 percent of the home's purchase price to the other partner, Chris, and is on the hook for gift tax and for filing a gift tax return. If Pat dies first, the home is entirely included in her estate, unless Chris can show contributions to purchase. And in a surprising twist of fate, the entire value of the home will also be included in Chris' estate when she dies. If that sounds like double-dipping, well, it is.

Income Tax

Obviously, an unmarried couple can't file a joint return or married filing separately return. This may save or cost money, depending upon the relative incomes of the life partners. Many regulations set limits based on filing status, and all of these are affected by the inability to for an unmarried couple to file a joint return. For example, certain income limits apply to the deductibility of traditional IRA contributions and to the ability to contribute to a Roth IRA. Those limits are higher for joint filers.

Certain deductions are available to joint-filing spouses. For example, a spouse can deduct the qualified educational and medical expenses of the other spouse. Unmarried couples must take their own deductions, which can be costly if the student or ill partner happens to have little or no income. A married couple that works together can file taxes as a sole proprietorship, but this option is not available to non-married partners who share a business.

A spouse is exempt from paying taxes on the health benefits received from the other spouse's job. An unmarried partner must treat the benefit as income. Under the Affordable Care Act, each non-married partner must own a separate health insurance policy, which is normally more expensive than the amount a married couple would spend on the same coverage through a family policy.

Trusts and Wills

Trusts are an important tool of financial planning. They can also be exceedingly convoluted, and we can but briefly touch on the subject. But a few special cases merit discussion:

• Grantor Retained Income Trust (GRIT): The grantor funds the trust, receives the net income from the trust's assets for a stated period, and then the remaining assets, including appreciation, passes to the beneficiary. Business owners can use this scheme for succession planning by placing up to 49 percent of a business into the trust. A peculiarity of the trust is that the assets passed to the beneficiary may be assessed at less than fair market value, thereby reducing the gift tax. A second peculiarity is that the beneficiary can't be a spouse or relative. Therefore, while this trust is useful for non-married couples, same-sex couples who get married and are also parties to this trust might have a problem on their hands. Seek qualified advice.

• Charitable Lead Annuity Trust (CLAT): This is useful when an individual, the grantor, wants to provide for the financial security of a non-spouse partner after the death of the grantor. A CLAT allows the grantor to take an immediate tax deduction on the assets contributed. The trust will annually distribute funds to qualified charities until the grantor's death, at which time the remainder passes to the surviving partner.

• If you want your unmarried partner to inherit your wealth, by all means create a will naming the partner as beneficiary. If you die intestate, the inheritance might go to a distant relative you despise rather than to your beloved life partner.

• An inheritance to a surviving spouse usually avoids probate, a time-consuming and costly affair. An unmarried couple can work around the problems via living trusts, transfer-on-death accounts, registrations, deeds and joint ownership arrangements — all require the services of an expert to set up correctly.

Using a Financial Planner

We've just briefly surveyed some of the financial planning considerations that non-traditional couples must address. Many more special situations can arise, and it seems like every one of them is unique in some way. By retaining the services of a financial planner who has expertise handling the needs of non-traditional couples, you receive important guidance for you particular circumstances, plus all the benefits that any client would receive — planning for investments, wealth accumulation, taxes, retirement, estates, gifting, trusts and more. Rick DiBiasio is a Certified Financial Planner™ with more than 30 years of experience seeing to the financial needs of all kinds of clients, and is available to assist same-sex couples and other non-traditional partners in structuring their finances for maximum benefit.

The Book Ends, and Your Retirement Begins

When I began to write this book, I set out to answer some of the most common questions that I run into as a retirement planning specialist. My practice, in Windermere, Fl. is based squarely around financial planning for those getting ready to retire, and I hoped, as I wrote this to you, that you would feel like you were having dinner conversation with a trusted friend. My clients, who are located throughout the country, tell me that I can make complicated financial information understandable, and I appreciate that. Wall Street often seems to go out of its way to portray itself as the keeper of wisdom, who only condescends to talk to mere mortals from wood paneled offices designed to flaunt their financial superiority.

"Pay no attention to the man behind the curtain!"

I'll leave you with this notion: your set of retirement questions might be similar to someone else's, but in fact, they are unique, and if you run into someone who has a computer program, a free lunch seminar, or some other pre-packaged retirement solution, I urge you to run. The Wall Street money machine has become one giant algorithm designed to separate you from your money by applying statistics about the world in general to you in particular. The first thing you learn in a college statistics class is that statistics don't apply to individuals; and just as the 12 signs of the Zodiac can't accurately predict your day (or the rest of the 1/12th of the world's population that shares your sign), a pre-packaged retirement solution is probably not going to apply to you.

When it comes to retirement investing, there truly is no such thing as a free lunch, so before you go to a free luncheon or dinner "workshop" to hear some financial guy's sales pitch, ask yourself a simple question: why is he investing all of his marketing dollars on expensive mailers and dinner at a fine steak house? I'll answer that one for you: because it makes business sense. He's putting many dollars in one end of his pipeline and taking many more dollars out on the other end. I'm not against financial advisors making money, I'm against one-size-fits- all investment solutions and the herd mentality that goes with investing. You can't outperform other investors is you are investing the same way that they do, and you can't invest differently from other investors if you are following the same advice that they are.

I wrote The Retirement Dilemma because I truly believe that we are at a crucial crossroads for our entire generation, if you don't take a measured, sober, and realistic look at your retirement investment strategy before you retire, you will be forced to do so after you retire. The Bins and Gaps approach to retirement planning may not paint the rosiest picture of retirement, but I guarantee you that it gives you a realistic way to plan to stay retired. By matching your assets to both your budget and your life expectancy, and then taking a longer term view of investing, you are removing all but the most systematized risk from your portfolio.

In my practice, I value my independence: I work as a finan-cial advisor, not a as a product representative, so I have no stake in the game as to which investments I recommend, I am on the same side of the table as my clients. It has been my experience that, in the long run, investment selection is not as important as a patient, disciplined approach to investing and this philosophy becomes significantly easier when you remove the short term assets in your portfolio from the day to day fluctuations of the financial markets. It's also been my experience that there is no shortage of good financial oppor-tunities, and there is never, ever any reason to invest before you are comfortable with the investment you are thinking of purchasing.

Don't be in a rush.

The decisions that you are about to make about your retirement assets are not to be taken lightly, a well-designed portfolio can distribute risk, provide an inflation hedge, and give you the growth that is necessary to fund your retire-ment. There is no reason to listen to a security sales-person's urgent pleas to invest now because he or she believes that you have a "great opportunity" if you buy today. There are always good buys out there, in fact, it is usually a good idea to invest slowly, and systematically, to dollar cost average into all of you positions. Again, I believe in a long-term view.

I hope that you have found the information I've presented to you to be useful. I invite you to visit my firm's website, especially my blog, where we keep videos and articles to fur-ther help explain the concepts presented in *The Retirement Dilemma*. It's my further hope that you have a wonderfully successful retirement and that maybe someday we will run into one another on the bike trail, on a tour of some ancient city, or here in Florida.

THANKS,

Rick DiBiasio
Certified Financial Planner Practitioner.

www.latitudesfinancial.com

ABOUT THE AUTHOR

Rick DiBiasio is a Certified Financial Planner™, an avid bicyclist, an author and a less than adequate guitarist. He is also a professional speaker, a comedic improvisation performer, and a puller of weeds. He is the husband of Teresa DiBiasio, a father of 4, and Grandfather of 4 (so far.) He is the author of *The Affluent Artist* (with a forward by Jack Canfield) and *When Do I Get to Be Me?*

Made in the USA
Columbia, SC
01 June 2018